CLINICAL PS   LOGY
AND   ICE

CLINICAL PSYCHOLOGY AND SINGLE-CASE EVIDENCE

A Practical Approach to Treatment Planning and Evaluation

Franz Petermann
Jörg M. Müller

JOHN WILEY & SONS, LTD
Chichester · New York · Weinheim · Brisbane · Singapore · Toronto

Other Wiley Editorial Offices

John Wiley & Sons, Inc., 605 Third Avenue,
New York, NY 10158-0012, USA

WILEY-VCH GmbH, Pappelallee 3,
D-69469 Weinheim, Germany

John Wiley Australia Ltd, 33 Park Road, Milton,
Queensland 4064, Australia

John Wiley & Sons (Asia) Pte Ltd, 2 Clementi Loop #02-01,
Jin Xing Distripark, Singapore 129809   I00S862184

John Wiley & Sons (Canada) Ltd, 22 Worcester Road,
Rexdale, Ontario M9W 1L1, Canada

Library of Congress Cataloging-in-Publication Data

Petermann, Franz.
    Clinical psychology and single-case evidence : a practical approach to treatment
planning and evaluation / Franz Petermann, Jörg M. Müller.
        p. cm.
    Includes bibliographical references (p.) and index.
    ISBN 0-471-49156-X (cased) — ISBN 0-471-49157-8 (pbk.)
    1. Psychotherapy—Evaluation.   2. Psychotherapy—Planning.   3. Single subject
research.   4. Clinical psychology.   I. Müller, Jörg M.   II. Title.

RC480.5 .P47 2001
616.89'14—dc21

                                                                2001022516

British Library Cataloguing in Publication Data

A catalogue record for this book is available from the British Library

ISBN 0-471-49156-X (cloth)
ISBN 0-471-49157-8 (paper)

Typeset in 11/13pt Palatino by Dorwyn Ltd, Rowlands Castle, Hants.
Printed and bound in Great Britain by Biddles Ltd, Guildford and King's Lynn
This book is printed on acid-free paper responsibly manufactured from sustainable
forestry, in which at least two trees are planted for each one used for paper production.

CONTENTS

LIST OF FIGURES

LIST OF TABLES

ABOUT THE AUTHORS

Prof. Dr. Franz Petermann, born in 1953, studied mathematics and psychology at the University of Heidelberg. He achieved his PhD in 1977; since 1980 he has held professorships for Clinical Psychology at the Universities of Berlin, Bonn and Bremen. Director of the Centre for Rehabilitation Research at the University of Bremen since 1996, his main research interests are psychological diagnostic, clinical child psychology and rehabilitation research.

Dipl. Psych. Jörg Michael Müller, born in 1968, studied psychology at the University of Heidelberg. He was a lecturer at the College for Speech Therapy at the University of Heidelberg and research assistant at the University of Heidelberg Poliklinik from 1997 to 1998. Since 1998 he has been research assistant and statistical consultant at the Center for Rehabilitation Research, University of Bremen. His research interests are methodology and evaluation.

PREFACE

The focus of this book is on methods of controlled practice as a means of evidence-based, clinical decision-making and intervention with single cases. In 'controlled practice' psychotherapists and patients are partners who cooperate for continuous optimization of psychotherapies. Since this concept may not have received full recognition in the Anglo-American world, this book offers an opportunity to become acquainted with it.

The application of single-case analysis to the field of quality assurance lends particular significance to this book. Quality criteria need to meet certain specific demands arising from the relationship between therapist and patient. Psychotherapist and patient jointly define the meaning of 'quality' and 'success'. From our point of view, the purposeful use of standardized questionnaires is often limited with single cases. Too nonspecific and time-consuming, they usually fail to address the more particular features of the presented problems. Therefore, we present new ways of describing the problem and therapy as well as the analysis.

After having completed the book, a discussion of single-case studies in clinical research was published in an article by Fishman (2000). In present this topic is considered highly actual (Seligman, 2000; Stricker, 2000). These articles reflect the importance of a single case analysis within an improvement and control of clinical practice. Therefore we hope to be able give our readers a technical guideline.

We would like to express our gratitude to Dr. G. Groen for his valuable support and comments. Dr. Hans C. Waldmann contributed the chapter 'Statistical analysis'. Dr. T. Kroll helped too improve the English language adaptation. We wish to thank everyone involved in the production of this book—especially John Wiley & Sons Ltd and in particular Editorial Assistant Lesley Valerio—for their patience and cooperation, and also Dr. Michael Bruch of University College London, who suggested the idea of the English edition to the publishers. With this book we hope to provide a variety of new and helpful ideas for psychotherapists and patients.

Bremen, April 2000   Franz Petermann
                                                 Jörg M. Müller

Chapter 1

INTRODUCTION

1.1 WHY DO WE NEED A CONTROLLED PRACTICE?

Clinical practice finds itself confronted with budgeting constraints on the one hand and consumer protection laws requiring optimization of health care performance on the other (see, for example, President Clinton's speech on the 'Consumer Bill of Rights and Responsibilities', March 1997). Until now, traditional psychotherapy research has hardly met these demands, and its impact on clinical practice has remained limited (Barlow, 1981; Garfield, 1982; Smith, Glass & Miller, 1980). However, the focus of quality control in the field of mental health (care) increasingly shifts from monitoring service structure toward greater control on psychotherapists' work. Therefore, it seems necessary to ask how quality control can be best accomplished in clinical practice. At this point the lack of a theory-based framework for integrating methods of data collection and analysis with actual therapy becomes evident. The empirical nature of controlled practice complements non-empirical methods of quality assurance such as peer supervision.

The concept of controlled practice was first introduced in a German publication by Petermann in 1982, in which he examined the realization of scientific demands in psychotherapeutic practice. Barlow (1981) recognized the potential of the single-case approach (or 'intensive local observation' as Cronbach (1975) called it) to influence clinical practice, since it seeks to answer 'why' and 'how' something is happening rather than looking at 'who' is involved 'where' (Yin, 1984). Controlled practice fits into the tradition of the Scientific-Practitioner Models as proposed by the American Psychological Association: 'Clinical psychologists are scientists who evaluate their work and their theories with rigor and practitioners who utilize a research-based understanding of human behavior in social contexts to aid people in resolving psychological dysfunction and enhancing their lives' (Kendall, Flannery-Schroeder & Ford, 1999: 331). Controlled practice represents a compromise between scientifc demands for exactness—which are deemed unrealistic in clinical practice research—and the intuition of many clinicians to 'want to help only'.

1.2   THE SCOPE OF THIS BOOK

Single-case analysis, as part of a controlled-practice approach, can serve various interests. While some therapists might be interested only in documenting their therapies, others may wish to give their patients feedback on the progress made during therapy. As emphasized in learning theory, feedback plays an important role in behavior modification by relating experiences of self-efficacy to patients. In that way, feedback is a part of therapy and can thus enhance the patients' motivation and their compliance (with treatment). In addition, it is a methodological approach that assists therapists in evaluating and revising their interventions throughout the therapeutic process.

However, the most important advantage of controlled practice is that therapists obtain feedback on their *own* behavior as a basis for continuous optimization. Primarily, therapists need to document the therapy and explain their working theory in order to evaluate fit and misfit of plans, actions and results (see Chapter 8). As Kanfer and Goldstein (1991) point out, 'It's only with such documentation that helper and client can decide whether the change program has been effective, and further decisions about shifting to other objectives or terminating the relationship can be made' (p. 14).

1.3   PREREQUISITES OF CONTROLLED PRACTICE

Systematic single-case analysis has to meet certain demands and can be quite time-consuming. This book was written with the intention of providing the necessary 'know-how' in single-case methodology. Most initial difficulties will be overcome when therapists become familiar with the practice evaluation 'tools' over time and have implemented evaluation strategies as routines. Depending on individual knowledge and prior experiences, time requirements may differ from estimates shown in Table 1.1; nevertheless these figures can serve as an initial frame of reference, helping therapists to decide whether they are willing to make the necessary time investment.

Table 1.1   Time requirements per case

Planning the single-case evaluation with the patient	1 hour
Data collection and entry	2 hours
Data analysis (data verification, description, tables, graphs)	2 hours
Application (comparison of similar cases)	1 hour
Total	6 hours

How a single-case analysis is to be performed exactly depends not only on the fulfillment of some general requirements (see section 3.4) but also on certain abilities of the patient. Of particular importance are self-monitoring and reflecting skills as well as the compliance of the patient. In some situations, for example acute crisis intervention with patients seeking help for acute stress disorder (DSM-IV, Code 308.3), collecting data from the patient creates an additional burden to that person which should be avoided as a general rule. In these circumstances alternative ways of collecting data need to be identified (e.g. reference from relatives or peers). In some instances, it may be sufficient if the therapist thoroughly documents the therapeutic process.

1.4   CHAPTER OVERVIEW

This book begins with a detailed overview of quality assurance strategies. It is argued from a historical perspective that controlled practice constitutes a necessary development (Chapter 2). In Chapter 3 we will show how treatment planning and interventions can be linked to the methodology of single-case analysis. In this chapter we will also address some technical problems of integrating single-case evaluation with the therapy process without interfering interventions. Chapter 4 covers the ever-changing significance of single-case methodology throughout the history of psychology. This chapter also includes a section on the importance of psychotherapy research as a major source of technological knowledge for single-case analysis. In Chapter 5 we present a detailed example (from clinical practice) and discuss necessary, additional steps to conduct controlled-practice evaluation.

Chapters 6 through 11 address specific aspects of controlled practice. In Chapter 6 we suggest the use of graphic representations to describe client problems, while Chapter 7 not only shows how graphs can be used to illustrate working theories, but also shows that graphical treatment explanations can serve as a basis for treatment planning. In Chapter 8 we discuss the use of therapy process questionnaires and encourage therapists to develop their own case- and symptom-specific instruments. Aspects on how to define the focus of an analysis and how to formulate hypotheses about change are introduced in Chapter 9. Additionally in this chapter there are hints on how to prepare the answers for data processing, while the data analysis is explained in more detail in Chapter 10. Finally, Chapter 11 stresses the advantages of controlled practice as a documentation and data storage system.

Chapter 2

QUALITY ASSURANCE IN MENTAL HEALTH

2.1 ABOUT THIS CHAPTER

In this chapter controlled practice is introduced as a method of quality assurance in mental health. Quality assurance (QA) is considered on three levels:

- structural level, i.e. the health care system
- process level, i.e. treatment of a patient
- personal level, i.e. the therapist as a person

Donabedian (1966) was first to distinguish structure, process, and person. There are different procedures of QA on each level (see Table 2.1). Controlled practice is a method of process level QA parallel to actual intervention, and does rely on the case study approach for documentation.

In this chapter the following topics will be discussed:

- Definition of quality
- Comments on the historical development of quality assurance
- Quality assurance at the health care provider level
- Quality assurance at treatment level

Table 2.1 Organization of quality assurance in mental health

Level (Donabedian, 1966)	Mental health	Quality assurance
Structure	Health care system	Accreditation
Process	Treatment	Methods of controlled practice Supervision Therapy manuals
Person	Therapist	Education and approbation

Controlled practice as a method of quality assurance in therapy will be considered in Chapter 3.

2.2   DEFINITION OF QUALITY

Any form of QA is based on the definition of the term 'quality'. Quality is not a tangible entity. According to the International Organization for Standardization (ISO, standard 9000, see Box 2.1), quality refers to the assessment of the manufacturing process of a product or a service.

Box 2.1   What is ISO 9000 ?

The ISO 9000 family of standards represents an international consensus on good management practices with the aim of ensuring that the organization can, time and time again, deliver product or services that meet the client's quality requirements. These good practices have been distilled into a set of standardized requirements for a quality management system, regardless of your organization's size, what it does, or whether it's in the private, or public sector.

Source: ISO; http://www.tc176.org/faqs/index.html; 17.2.2000

Accordingly, it is always the consumer who must decide whether a product or service does or does not live up to the expected standard. When a blacksmith uses a hammer to bring a hook into the desired shape, he has to make sure that the iron is hot enough and that iced water is available to cool the glowing iron. If he abides by these and other rules of the manufacturing process, the final product will have the desired properties, such as a high degree of hardness and durability. On the other hand, if the manufacturing process is uncoordinated and the product quality happened by chance, it is impossible to guarantee that the product will live up to manufacturing and outcome standards. It does not matter whether an individual could produce an excellent hook every now and then, because no one will place trust in a manufacturer whose products are only occasionally of high quality. The blacksmith must demonstrate again and again that he is capable of following the rules and attaining the desired quality standards if he expects customers to have trust in the product. Quality assurance is therefore a continuing process, and Box 2.2 defines its essential features.

Box 2.2   Defining quality in terms of a manufacturing process

The manufacturing process is the basis of assigning quality attributes to a product or service. Quality is related to the manufacturing processes that are guaranteed for a particular product. A manufacturing process follows unambiguous rules which allow replication. Describing these rules constitutes the foundation for evaluating quality. A single test of a production process is not sufficient to assure the quality of future products. Thus an ongoing evaluation, parallel to the manufacturing process, is necessary.

Figure 2.1 presents general practice guidelines for the development of quality assurance standards. These standards, known as ISO 9000, are 'generic'. 'Generic means that the same standards can be applied to any organization, large or small, whatever its product—including whether its "product" is actually a service – in any sector of activity, and whether it is a business enterprise, a public administration, or a government department' (from: http://www.iso.ch/9000e/generic.htm.)

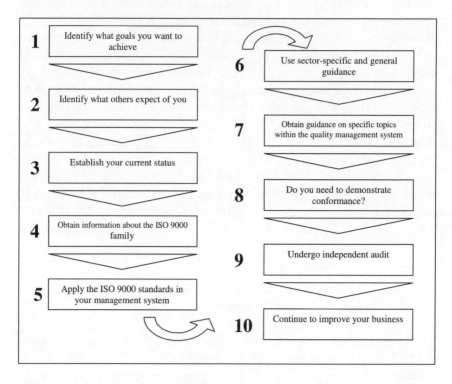

Figure 2.1 Selection and use of ISO 9000 (ISO, 1998) (http://www.iso.ch/9000e/9k14e.htm; 17.2.2000)

The definition of expectations (see 1 and 2 in Figure 2.1) and the description of the actual process are of particular interest. Transferred to the *structural level* of mental health, these steps may address issues of access to and availability of particular types of health care (e.g. 1, goals of the health care provider). Surveys assessing customer needs and demands regarding the provision of health care services (expectation of the consumer) contrast the offered services (see section 2.2). The section 'Quality assurance at structural level' contains a comprehensive listing of such aims and expectations.

At *treatment level*, the patient's primary interest relates to clarity in the treatment process and outcome prognosis.

At the *personal level*, practice guidelines such as the practitioner credentials of the American Psychology Association (APA)—on the web: http://www.apa.org/practice/psych.html—state criteria for the qualification of psychologists. These guidelines also include information on accredited care plans.

To elucidate the objectives and demands of health care providers and consumers at the three levels of QA, the following questions may be asked (see also Figure 2.1, steps 1 through 3):

- What are the health care provider's demands?
- To what extent are the patient's needs considered?
- What conditions are imperative for 'best' practice?
- How can the treatment or service be evaluated?
- Is it possible to (a) plan, (b) document, and (c) evaluate the treatment process?

Every therapist can try to find answers to these questions. The last question may be answered by employing controlled-practice strategies.

In Figure 2.1, items 4 through 7 draw the attention to additional sources of information of ISO and to guidelines. Item 8 requires demonstration that procedures comply with quality norms, while item 9 calls for external evaluation. This phase will be described in more detail in the section 'Quality assurance at the healthcare provider level'.

2.3   COMMENTS ON THE HISTORICAL DEVELOPMENT OF QUALITY ASSURANCE

In the following the historical development of QA will be outlined briefly, before attention is turned to QA measures at the three levels. The history of QA in mental health care highlights the limitations of contemporary QA.

Attitudes toward and treatments for people with mental health problems have changed profoundly during the last two centuries. However, some disadvantages and stigmatization have prevailed into our days or become even more pronounced (Phelan et al., 1997). Primarily, changes have occurred in terms of:

(a) definition of mental illness,
(b) primary treatment setting
(c) types of treatment.

The role of diagnostics in the context of quality assurance

In the early days of psychiatry, classification systems for mental conditions were virtually non-existent, and diagnoses were merely 'labels' without clear-cut definitions. Physicians followed basic observational customs and made their diagnoses on the grounds of social attributions rather than on medical evidence. Society as a whole rejected the 'abnormal', and has in many ways remained anxious to keep people with mental difficulties at a distance (Star, 1952, 1955; Gurin, Veroff & Feld, 1960; Veroff, Douvan & Kulka, 1981). In Germany, Karl Jaspers (1883–1969) and Kurt Schneider (1887–1967) were the founding fathers of 'descriptive phenomenological psychiatry', which had as one of its main goals the systematizing of psychopathology. Theirs were the first attempts to develop a nosology, or classification system, in order to improve the treatment of psychiatric patients. Emil Kraepelin (1856–1926) and Eugen Bleuler (1857–1939) introduced such terms as 'exogenous' and 'endogenous' psychosis or 'schizophrenia', which still feature in contemporary classifications of psychopathology. These efforts may be considered an important first step toward quality assurance. A classification system of diagnoses is fundamental to QA since timely and appropriate treatment is impossible in the absence of a clear definition of the condition (e.g. an identification of clinical symptoms and their causes). It is also needed in order to systematically evaluate and improve psychological therapies.

The role of institutions in quality assurance

Let us now examine the role of institutions in the development of mental health. In the middle of the 18th century, the first 'asylums' for people with mental health problems emerged in the United States (Grob, 1983, 1991, 1994), where until then most mentally challenged people lived with their families. In many other countries, such as France and Britain, asylums had been in existence for quite some time. Most 18th-century institutions treated inmates in a degrading and condescending manner. Accommodation of these unfortunate people in prison-like facilities can be explained in part by a lack of funding. Then, in a historic decree in 1794, the French physician Philippe Pinel (1745–1826) released the 'insane' at the Hospice de Bicetre from their chains and cleared the way for more humane and caring attitudes and behavior toward people with mental disorders. In 1908 former patient Clifford Beers instigated another development by his book *A Mind that Found Itself* (1908), a narrative of his own experiences with psychiatric care. Beers later co-founded the National Committee on Mental Hygiene (NCMH), which also advocated more humane interaction with people with mental health problems. The NCMH was a precursor of the National Mental Health Association (NMHA).

Table 2.2 Historical reform movements in mental health treatment in the United States (modified from Morrissey and Goldman (1985) and Goldman and Morrissey (1985))

Reform movement	Era	Setting	Focus of reform
Moral treatment	1800–1850	Asylum	Humane, restorative treatment
Mental hygiene	1890–1920	Mental hospital or clinic	Prevention, scientific orientation
Community mental health	1955–1970	Community mental health center	Deinstitutionalization, social integration
Community support	1975–present	Community support	Mental illness as a social welfare problem (e.g. housing, employment)
Quality assurance	1995–present	Quality Assurance Center	Controlling the needs, costs and quality-of-treatment-relation.

Table 2.2 lists various reform movements and reorientations that stimulated the practice of mental health care (e.g. community integration). The most recent trend in QA lies with the move toward greater patient emancipation and a redefinition of the patient as a consumer in the health care system.

The structural development of the US national health system can be expressed not only in terms of changed attitudes on the part of the public and the medical profession, but also in the rise of institutions that had a profound impact on mental health legislation. A summary of the history of such legal initiatives and regulations can be found on the website of the National Institutes of Health (NIH; http://www.nih.gov/welcome/almanac/main.html) and the National Institute of Mental Health (NIMH; http://www.nih.gov/welcome/almanac/historical-data/chronology.html) (see also Box 2.3).

Table 2.3   Development of NIH and NIMH

1879	The National Board of Health was created by law. It represented the first organized, comprehensive, national medical research effort of the Federal Government.
1912	The name Public Health and Marine Hospital Service was changed to Public Health Service (PHS).
1946	Establishment of a National Institute of Mental Health.
1963	Mental Retardation Facilities and Community Mental Health Centers (CMHC), beginning a new era in Federal support for mental health services.
1968	NIMH became a component of PHS's Health Services and Mental Health Administration (HSMHA).

Source: NIH 1999 Almanac; http://www.nih.gov/about/almanac/index.html; 17.2.2000

These institutional changes bore heavily on staking out the government's responsibility in promoting health services and evaluation research. The Community of Mental Health Centers (CMHC) was at the center of this development. In the Federal Regulation for the CMHCs Act of 1965, CMHCs were ordered to allocate a certain amount of public funding to evaluation purposes.

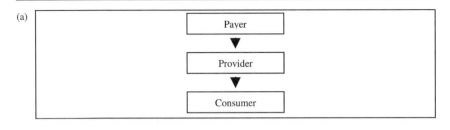

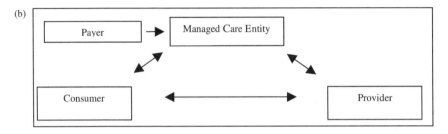

Figure 2.2   The context of quality assurance (Lyons, et al., 1997: 4ff)

In the 1980s managed care was introduced in the US health care system, leading to a transformation in health care delivery. The immediate cause for establishing care-controlling measures was the pressing need to stop the unrelenting growth in health care expenditure. As a consequence, relationships among health care providers, health insurers, purchasers and consumers of health care products have changed dramatically (see Figure 2.2). Decision-making power in clinical practice has shifted away from health care providers to managed care organizations, which have widely replaced the traditional fee-for-service system in which health care providers were retrospectively reimbursed for their services. In managed care, most services are restricted (i.e. only a limited type and number of diagnostic tests and treatments are refunded). Access to specialists and mental health care providers are regulated by primary care physicians or nurses who function as 'gatekeepers'. Excessive service utilization is discouraged. Various studies have shown that consumers enrolled in managed care insurance plans are less satisfied with their care and perceive access to specialist health care as more problematic than people enrolled in traditional indemnity plans (Center for Studying Health Systems Change, 2000). As a result of the dominating influence of managed care organizations, or HMOs (Health Maintenance Organizations), health care providers have organized in so-called provider networks in order to bolster their negotiating power for provider contracts with the HMOs and to develop integrative models of health care provision.

Consumer organizations are increasingly voicing their discontent with current mental health practice (Lefley, 1996). Voluntary pressure groups and associations such as the Mental Patients' Liberation Movement (Chamberlin, 1995) seek to influence health policy decision making. Other examples are the National Alliance for the Mentally Ill, the National Association of Mental Patients, and the National Mental Health Consumers' Association. A federal register, encompassing all 50 states and the District of Columbia, lists 235 different mental health consumer organizations (South Carolina SHARE, 1995). Apart from these national groups, various patient associations and self-help groups also exist. Their aim is not so much to bring about structural changes in the health care system as to provide mutual support and advice. Some authors (DeJong & Sutton, 1995) have argued that the empowerment of the consumers will eventually lead to another shift in the health care system, away from a payer-driven system toward a system driven by consumers and outcomes. Consumer magazines such as *Consumer Reports* contribute to the increasing participation of mental health care consumers in the debate about the care they receive.

Managed care has helped to control health care expenses, thus placing restrictions on health care providers. Apart from pursuing an economic-based interest in reforming the health care market, the research community has intensified its efforts to identify more effective and efficient treatments. New methods in diagnostics and treatment documentation allow for comparisons among different institutions and across treatment facilities (see section 4.6). Treatments themselves have evolved gradually over time, as will be shown in the next section.

The role of treatments and quality assurance

From today's point of view, the 18th century offered no effective treatment for mental illness. People labeled 'lunatic' were subjected to 'educational practices' which, in the light of modern psychology and psychiatry, seem more like torture (e.g. swiveling chairs, ice-water dunks). These methods of returning patients to 'sanity' were coupled with practices of declaring individuals mentally incompetent to take care of their own affairs and of imposing massive restrictions on their civil rights. These practices were first seriously challenged by Philippe Pinel of France (1745–1826) and John Corolly of England (1794–1866). Their 'nonrestraint' movement slowly brought about a change in attitudes that finally led to a greater emphasis on communication with psychiatric patients as a central component in their treatment.

Psychoanalysis, developed by Sigmund Freud (1856–1936), marked the birth of communication-centered psychotherapy. For the first time, a theoretical framework attempted an integration of etiologic, diagnostic, and treatment-related concepts. Other therapy schools were soon to follow. In the United States, B.F. Skinner (1904–1990) developed behavioral therapy, based on learning theory. A trend of pluralism and diversification in the methods of psychotherapy led to greater choice for therapists and patients.

2.4   QUALITY ASSURANCE AT THE HEALTH CARE PROVIDER LEVEL

The last section will trace the developments that finally led to contemporary quality assurance in mental health, including systematic classification systems in diagnostics, emergence of modern treatment facilities, and method diversification of treatments.

Methods of QA at a structural level will first be described, including:

- Rights of mental health consumers
- Foundation of QA institutions and development of methods to evaluate mental health care plans
- Various sources of information (i.e. the Internet).

Box 2.3   Four major sectors of the mental health service system

(*Surgeon General's Report on Mental Health*, 1999;
http://www.nimh.nih.gov/mhsgrpt/chapter6/sec1.html
17.2.2000).

[1] The *specialty mental health sector* consists of mental health professionals such as psychiatrists, psychologists, psychiatric nurses, and psychiatric social workers who are trained specifically to treat people with mental disorders. The great bulk of specialty treatment is now provided in outpatient settings such as private office-based practices or in private or public clinics. Public sector facilities include state/county mental hospitals and multi-service mental health facilities, which often coordinate a wide range of outpatient, intensive case management, partial hospitalization, and inpatient

[2] The *general medical/primary care sector* consists of health care professionals such as general internists, pediatricians, and nurse practitioners in office-based practice, clinics, acute medical/surgical hospitals, and nursing homes.

[3] The *human services sector* consists of social services, school-based counseling services, residential rehabilitation services, vocational rehabilitation, criminal justice/prison-based services, and religious professional counselors.

[4] The *voluntary support network sector*, which consists of self-help groups, such as 12-step programs and peer counselors, is a rapidly growing component of the mental and addictive disorder treatment system.

Quality assurance will be considered primarily with regard to the first two areas of Box 2.3. Independent nonprofit organizations such as the National Committee for Quality Assurance (NCQA, http://www.ncqa.org/Pages/policy/accreditation/ppoaccred.htm)

offer information on QA standards and measurements. The NCQA also defines quality criteria that mental health providers must follow in order to become accredited managed care organizations. The NCQA awards certificates of excellence and grades providers as 'excellent', 'commendable', 'accredited', 'provisional', or 'denied', depending on the extent to which they comply with quality standards. Accreditation is based on audits and HEDIS (Health Plan Employer Data and Information Set) data. Findings on accreditation and the quality of care offered by different providers are available to consumers in Accreditation Summary Reports (see Box 2.4).

Box 2.4   Accreditation Summary Reports

Source: NCQA; http://www.ncqa.org/pages/info/asr.htm; 17.2.2000

Accreditation Summary Reports (ASRs) are short, user-friendly reports that show in detail how well a health plan performed on its NCQA accreditation survey. ASRs use bar graphs to demonstrate a plan's degree of compliance with NCQA's standards in each of the aspects of a health plan we investigate—quality improvement, credentialing, customer service, medical records, care management, and preventive health. ASRs give consumers and employers more detailed information about the strengths and weaknesses of individual health plans.

Box 2.5 shows six main evaluation categories for care plans in the accreditation process.

Box 2.5   NCQA's standards for quality NHPs

Source: NCQA; http://www.ncqa.org/pages/policy/accreditation/new%20health%20plan/newplan.htm

1. *Quality improvement*: What organizational structures and processes does the NHP have in place to monitor and improve the quality of care and service provided to its members? Does the NHP fully examine the quality of care given to its members? How well does the NHP coordinate all parts of its delivery system?

2. *Practitioner credentials*: Does the NHP meet specific NCQA requirements for investigating the training and experience of all practitioners in its network? Does the NHP look for any history of malpractice or fraud?

3. *Members' rights and responsibilities*: How clearly does the NHP inform members about how to access health services, how to choose a practitioner or change practitioners, and how to make a complaint? How responsive is the NHP to members' satisfaction ratings and complaints?

4. *Preventive health services*: Does the NHP encourage members to use its preventive health programs? Does the NHP encourage its practitioners to deliver preventive services?

5. *Utilization management*: Does the NHP use a reasonable and consistent process when deciding what health services are appropriate for individuals' needs? When the NHP denies payment for services, does it respond to member and practitioner appeals?

6. *Medical records:* How consistently do the medical records kept by the NHP's practitioners meet NCQA standards for quality care? For instance, do the records show that practitioners focus on treatment interventions that are consistent with treatment goals and objectives?

Recommendations concerning quality standards at the structural level are of particular interest for governmental organizations such as the Health Care Financing Administration (HCFA; http://www.hcfa.gov), which tracks the health care expenditures of the two public health care programs MEDICARE and MEDI-CAID. Apart from its economic focus, HCFA also responds to consumer demands and protects their rights. In his speech to the Advisory Commission on Consumer Protection and Quality in the Health Care Industry in March 1997, President Bill Clinton defined the organization's mission as 'to recommend such measures as may be necessary to promote and assure health care quality and value and protect consumers and workers in the health care system'. Since then, the Advisory Commission has formulated several guidelines on consumer protection (see Box 2.6).

Box 2.6   Quality and consumers' rights

Source: NIMH http://www.nimh.nih.gov/mhsgrpt/chapter6/appendix.html; 17.2.2000

The Consumer Bill of Rights and Responsibilities (Bill of Rights) is intended to meet three major goals:

[1] Strengthen consumer confidence by assuring that the health care system is fair and responsive to consumers' needs; it gives consumers credible and effective mechanisms for addressing their concerns and encourages them to take an active role in improving and assuring their health.

[2] Reaffirm the importance of a strong relationship between consumers and their health care professionals.

[3] Underscore the critical role of consumers in safeguarding their own health by establishing both rights and responsibilities for all participants in improving health status.

The guidelines in Box 2.6 can be used develop more concrete objectives (see Box 2.7).

Box 2.7   Measures of consumer protection and information

Source: NIMH; http://www.nimh.nih.gov/mhsgrpt/chapter6/
appendix.html; 17.2.2000

[1] Information disclosure of comparable measures of quality and consumer satisfaction from health plans, professionals, and facilities.

[2] Direct access to specialists of choice for consumers with complex or serious medical conditions who require frequent specialty care.

[3] Authorization, when required, for an adequate number of visits under an approved treatment plan.

[4] Vulnerable groups, including individuals with mental disabilities, require special attention by decision makers to protect their health coverage and quality of care.

[5] Confidentiality protections for sensitive services, such as mental health and substance abuse services, provided by health plans, providers, employers, and purchasers to safeguard against improper use or release of individually identifiable information.

[6] To move the mental health care system from a focus on providers to a focus on consumers, future care systems and quality tools will need to reflect person-centered values. This nascent trend is driven both by the Consumer Movement in American Society and by a strong focus on consumer rights in a managed care environment. First steps include the voluntary adoption of the principles of the Consumer Bill of Rights by Federal agencies and passage of legislation requiring their national implementation.

Public demand to give patients information on the effectiveness of treatments has been fulfilled partly by the new medium of the Internet.

Using new forms of information technology and communication:
the Internet

The Internet is an excellent new forum by which patients can gather information about treatments. It enables the consumer to gain fast, comprehensive, and inexpensive access to a wealth of medical knowledge. The significance of this new information technology for future QA in mental health care will depend on several factors:

First, access to this medium must not be restricted through barriers such as education, technology, and cost. Second, relevant information referring to the quality of treatments must be freely available. Until now, objective data are only insufficiently available online. Third, information must be both easily accessible and understandable to the consumer.

Some websites already provide consumers of health care services with a wide variety of information, for example Wellness-Health Care Information Resources (http://www-hsl.mcmaster.ca/tomflem/managed.html). Box 2.8 lists several well-designed and award-winning sites that cater to the information needs of health care consumers (see also MEDICARE information at http://www.hcfa.gov/medicare/mcarcnsm.html).

Box 2.8   Selected Internet links in mental health care

http://mentalhelp.net/

http://www.nimh.nih.gov/home.cfm

http://www.hcfa.gov/

http://www.cmhc.com/

http://www.ncqa.org/Pages/Main/index.htm

http://www.apa.org/psychnet/

Consumer information on symptoms, conditions, treatments and health care providers are currently available on the Internet. For example, someone wishing to find a psychotherapist in the local area can access the *Clinicians' Yellow Pages* (http://mentalhelp.net/mhn). Unfortunately, the credibility of 'professional pages' is frequently compromised by advertisements that promise help and advice but whose quality can hardly be evaluated by the consumer. Currently there are no control mechanisms in place to guide the selection of reliable sources of information.

It is almost certain that the wide range of current information of all shades of quality will eventually give way to fewer, more powerful, selective sources. Especially information platforms such as the Mental Health Net, imposing limitations of information overload, ought to have first priority in order to maintain its appeal and usefulness for consumers. The Internet's potential in the area of QA lies primarily within the ability to enable fast exchange of information. Therefore, it improves health care access only indirectly. The Internet also opens up new possibilities in the area of online treatment (telemedicine). Here it could become an arena for testing new interventions in therapy and patient education. While the Internet may prove a useful tool for providing information on the quality of health care, actual evaluation and modification of care programs will have to be implemented in the institutions that actually do provide the care. Patient councils in the Netherlands are a good example of how patients can establish a feedback system in their communication with health care providers.

In this section we have discussed the role of the patient/consumer in quality assurance as well as criteria for the evaluation of health care plans and the applicability of the Internet as a communication tool for the dialog between consumers and health professionals. In the following section, we will describe the psychotherapist's position in more detail. In particular we will discuss how therapists can meet the expectations and needs of clients on the one hand and satisfy QA demands on the other. What facilities does the therapist actually need to examine in order to improve the quality of treatment?

2.5   QUALITY ASSURANCE AT TREATMENT LEVEL

This section addresses the therapist's opportunities to maintain and improve the quality of psychotherapeutic care. Basic problems of quality assurance in psychotherapy are mostly due to limitations in the degree of standardization of classification and treatment of mental health problems.

Classification systems such as the ICD-10 or the DSM-IV have been developed to serve diverse purposes. For example, they may facilitate communication between health insurance companies and psychotherapists. Clinical syndromes and disorders are coded in terms of their primary symptoms. It is common, however, that not all aspects of a disorder which are relevant for therapy are covered by a classification. Disorder classification can be important for defining clear treatment indications and for planning the therapy; nevertheless, further information on causal and maintaining factors of a disorder is needed. Since this type of information cannot easily be standardized, individual problem analysis remains a necessity (see also Chapter 6).

The specification of treatment indications allows for a closer match of therapeutic interventions and specific disorders. Insufficient standardization of interventions that have to meet the individual needs of a client's diagnosis presents another problem. Even training packages still allow a considerable degree of flexibility in the way they are carried out. The lack of standardized procedures makes quality assurance difficult, since it is not always clear which step in the therapy is expected to produce which result. Treatment manuals are valuable tools in the evaluation of therapies because they spell out each procedure and its anticipated outcome in detail (Wilson, 1996; Kazdin, 1997; Garfield, 1998; Chambless & Hollon, 1998; Calhoun et al., 1998; Borkovec & Castonguay, 1998; Beutler, 1998).

Treatment manuals (if empirically supported) contain essential knowledge about empirically tested, successful therapeutic strategies. Unfortunately, these programs are often the result of a consen·ıs among therapists and lack sound empirical evidence. Recent developments in this area, such as the Oxford University's

Evidence-Based Mental Health project (EBMH; http://www. psychiatry.ox.co.uk/cebmh/frames.html) pursue the goal of systematizing clinical decision making on the basis of empirical evidence. The EBMH is a subdivision of Evidence-Based Medicine (Cochrane Library) which forms together with Evidence-Based Practice (EBP) group the Evidence-Based Health Care project (EBHC; http:www.uic.edu/depts/lib/health/hw/ebhc/; http://www. ihs.ox.ac.uk/ebhc/). These organizations publish only significant results from controlled studies. The study findings are used to develop evidence-based clinical practice guidelines

(http://www.uic.edu/depts/lib/health/hw/ebhc/journals.html).

Special emphasis is placed on presenting brief and understandable results so that clinical practitioners can use them in practice. A logical continuation to these EBMH practice guidelines are treatment manuals. However, such an approach may be problematic and raise the following questions:

(a) How can therapy be based on manuals, ignoring the specific characteristics of each individual case?

(b) How can psychotherapists be trained to use manuals effectively in clinical practice?

(c) Are manual-based therapies empirically superior to other types of therapies?

Skepticism among psychotherapists concerning rigid guidelines or manuals must not be underestimated. Referring to his experiences in medicine, Diamond (1998) concluded, 'You can drag physicians to guidelines . . . but you can't make them comply (mostly)'. There are many reasons for a lack of compliance among therapists. First, therapists may consider themselves to be the only ones with in-depth knowledge of the clients' situations and may feel that manuals do not sufficiently address the specific problems encountered. Second, therapists working in collaboration with other health professionals may have to meet certain standards and regulations (e.g. with regard to referral patterns or finances) and to abide by the 'philosophical traditions' of the institution. Third, ethical concerns that the special relationship between therapists and patients would be compromised may also limit the willingness to disclose details about a therapy. Fourth, there may be concerns about external control and interference. Fifth, psychotherapists ususally develop a unique set of skills or therapeutic 'styles' over time which may not combine well with manual-based interventions. Sixth, the necessity of changing well-established habits may reduce compliance. Finally, lack of evidence of the effectiveness of manual-based programs and problems with their implementation may preclude their use (Strupp, 1993; Alberts & Edelstein, 1990; Ford, 1979; Shiffman, 1987; Kendall, 1998).

Generally, the following question must be asked: 'To what degree, if any, can quality assurance in clinical practice be standardized?' It may be more useful to offer therapists a selection of QA strategies which they could match with the requirements of individual therapies. In addition to the controlled-practice method that will be described in detail in Chapter 3, peer supervision may be used as an element of QA, as this allows the therapist to discuss diagnostics and intervention strategies with experienced colleagues. So-called Balint groups (named after Michael Balint, 1896–1970) have proved to be very effective at prompting therapists in hospitals to discuss problematic interactions with their patients. Current developments in software technology facilitate planning and documentation of goals, strategies, and outcomes. The atomization of these tasks not only eases the burden for therapists but also makes clinical practice more efficient. Another aspect of QA is the continuing education and qualification of therapists.

In order to fulfill the ISO 9000 criteria, the consumer's perspective also needs to be considered. This aspect has not been considered satisfactorily in the QA strategies discussed in this chapter. Controlled practice, as a distinctive form of quality assurance, acknowledges the pivotal role of the patient.

Chapter 3

CONTROLLED PRACTICE AS QUALITY ASSURANCE

3.1 ABOUT THIS CHAPTER

In this chapter, controlled practice will be introduced as a method of quality assurance. Practical steps and methodological strategies will be presented in the following chapters. Here, we present a definition of controlled practice, a discussion of its objectives and functions, and turn to analyze the *linkage* of therapy and single-case methodology. We conclude with a discussion of the arguments made in favor of and against controlled practice.

Box 3.1   Definition of controlled practice

Controlled practice is the attempt to describe and document the therapeutic process with the help of single-case methodology in a practically relevant manner. It encompasses the definition and description of problem and therapy, the definition of process and outcome criteria, as well as data collection and documentation.

Monitoring and documenting the therapeutic process on the basis of a therapy contract is one of the main elements of controlled practice (see Figure 3.1).

Prior to monitoring, several demands have to be met.

- The clinical problem must be clearly defined and described (see Chapter 7, 'A graphical problem approach').

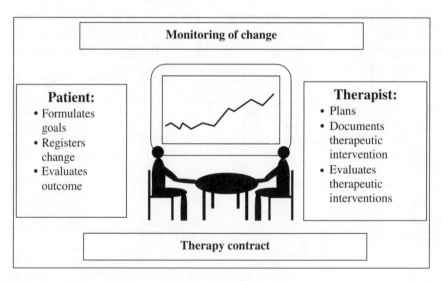

Figure 3.1   Monitoring the therapeutic process

- The patient needs to formulate goals in order to obtain criteria for success.
- Monitoring allows therapists to assess therapy-induced changes.
- Therapists need to devise a treatment plan (see Chapter 8, 'A graphical treatment approach') which allows for statements about the degree of expected change in particular outcome variables. The treatment plan also outlines the steps a therapist will take to help the patient achieve a positive outcome.

At the end of the therapy all interventions are evaluated, and it is very important that these additional demands for evaluation and monitoring are integrated in the therapeutic process.

After this rather rough overview, we will now discuss some topics in more detail. These include treatment integrity, monitoring, assessment of the therapy process by means of questionnaires, and the graphical presentation of data during the therapy process. Evaluating exactly how close therapists manage to translate treatment plans into action is a key aspect of quality assurance. The degree of correspondence between treatment plan and actual intervention is known as treatment integrity (Yeaton & Sechrest, 1981) (see also Box 3.2).

Box 3.2   Treatment integrity

Treatment integrity signifies the degree to which therapeutic actions reflect the treatment plan. Its evaluation requires an exact description of the chosen intervention. The more detailed the treatment can be described, and the more the therapist abides by the rules set out in the treatment plan, the higher is the level of treatment integrity.

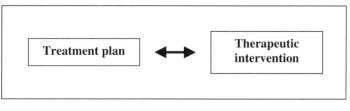

The pursuit of treatment integrity has consequences for treatment description. It should allow therapists to identify concrete therapeutic steps and intervention strategies must be easily discernible. Also, detailed documentation of therapy is of primary significance for the optimization of treatments. To approach this goal, therapists should be asked to state their intervention techniques and to document all changes made throughout the therapy process (see Chapter 8). Changes in patient behavior must also be documented—a process known as 'monitoring' (see Box 3.3).

Box 3.3   Monitoring

Monitoring refers to the registration of the therapy process using several different methods (e.g. self-reports, behavioral observations). Such ongoing evaluation highlights the patient's progress and relapse on central problem dimensions. Regular assessments, for example, with the help of diaries, enable both therapists and patients to respond to changes.

One of the best monitoring methods is a therapy process questionnaire which allows for comparisons over time. Process questionnaires ought to include items on current problem situation, behavior, cognition, and emotion. Answers are expected to reflect changes that are attributable to therapy, and patients should be asked to answer these short questionnaires repeatedly—if necessary, daily. (Box 3.4 shows an example).

If a patient's behavior and experiences are monitored for change over several weeks, a graphical representation of the data can facilitate systematic analysis (see Figure 3.2).

Timeplots demonstrate the patient's progress in a compact manner. If several variables are assessed, presentations may be stacked in order to give insight to temporal relationships. Expectations recorded prior to therapy can be compared with actual outcome. These may include therapist's assumptions and patient's expectations of the therapy.

Box 3.4 Change-sensitive questionnaire

Date:	Record ID:	Questionnaire Code:
	Quality of sleep	*I slept well last night*

1. *Very short* | –5 | –4 | –3 | –2 | –1 | 0 | 1 | 2 | 3 | 4 | 5 | *Very long*
2. *Restless* | –5 | –4 | –3 | –2 | –1 | 0 | 1 | 2 | 3 | 4 | 5 | *Rested*

	Mood	*Today, I feel . . .*

3. *Very bad* | –5 | –4 | –3 | –2 | –1 | 0 | 1 | 2 | 3 | 4 | 5 | *Very good*

4. *Very*
   dissatisfied | –5 | –4 | –3 | –2 | –1 | 0 | 1 | 2 | 3 | 4 | 5 | *Very*
   satisfied

. . .

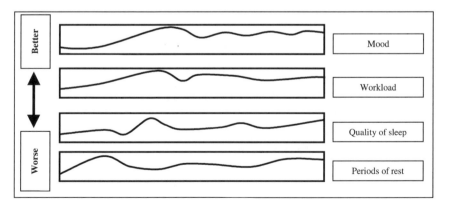

Figure 3.2 Graphical illustration of the therapy course

Monitoring and assessing therapeutic interventions are two essential features of controlled practice. They provide a systematic documentation of the therapist's interventions and ensuing changes in the patient. They render both therapy process and therapy outcome transparent to the patient; which might enhance his or her perception of self-efficacy, provided this outcome is deemed desirable. On the basis of evaluation, psychotherapists can control the chosen therapy plan, and, if necessary, revise the therapeutic approach systematically. Moreover, specific questions may be answered, such as:

- What feedback do I receive from my patient?
- What does my patient frequently criticize?
- What kind of patient am I most successful with?
- What should I keep especially in mind for future therapies?

Only the single-case approach can provide satisfactory answers to these questions, thus complementing other strategies of quality assurance (see Chapter 2). Psychotherapists have to decide for themselves whether they want to analyze the collected data personally or delegate this part of the practice evaluation to other experts. Among various options are specially designed software programs for psychotherapists and Internet-based data analysis services. In general, external service providers ensure a greater degree of analytic objectivity.

We will now describe how different therapeutic steps and their outcomes can be documented with the help of single-case analysis.

3.2   INTEGRATING THERAPY AND SINGLE-CASE EVIDENCE

We will now describe the documentation process in greater detail. In Figure 3.3 we divide therapy into seven steps to be linked to seven steps in single-case analysis. In both processes, four preparatory steps must be taken prior to actual therapy and its monitoring. Two steps conclude the process after completion of therapy.

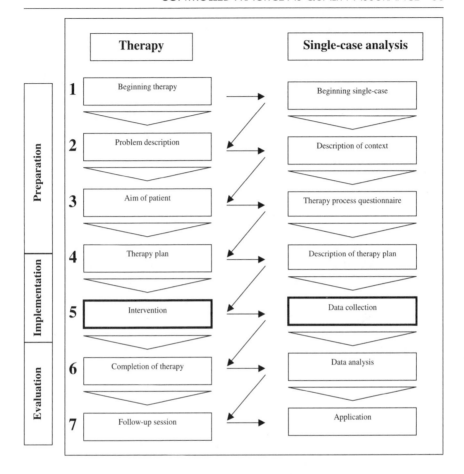

Figure 3.3   Parallel sequences of therapeutic intervention and single-case analysis

In Figure 3.3, arrows relate different steps in the therapy to steps in a single-case study. The direction of the arrows indicates that evaluation follows the specific circumstances of the therapy. Before we describe the different phases more thoroughly, we will explain the sequence in Figure 3.3. The right and left columns represent an idealized course of action and, in practice, it may be necessary to carry out some of these steps interactively. The therapeutic aims may change during the course of the therapy, thus necessitating a correction or adjustment of a therapy process questionnaire. As illustrated in Figure 3.3, therapy can be divided into three major parts: *preparation, implementation,* and *evaluation.* Therapy preparation encompasses problem description, diagnosis, development of a detailed therapy plan, and definition of specific outcome criteria. This information is used in designing a specific therapy questionnaire for the case study. It is very important that interventions or treatments are described in precise terms in order to interpret the outcomes correctly (see Box 3.5).

Box 3.5   Treatment

The description of treatment encompasses variables with impact on both cognition and behavior of the patient. For our purposes, treatment is meant to describe objectives, content, and strategies of psychotherapeutic interventions. All other factors that are not related to the intervention, while still influencing experiences and behaviors of a person, also need to be controlled.

Only when a therapy has been described and documented thoroughly can outcomes be shown to be attributable to the therapy. Single-case study methodology calls for a higher level of detail, exceeding the documentation requirements to which most therapists are accustomed. In turn, it allows the therapist to formulate expectations on the therapy process. The single-case approach makes the therapist's assumptions more precise by converting them into testable hypotheses.

Data are collected during the *implementation phase* (see Figure 3.3). Continuous data collection and analysis ensure that therapeutic interventions can be revised accordingly.

Progress, as a result of therapy, is assessed in the *evaluation phase.* The therapist reconsiders the course of intervention and optimizes therapy on the basis of direct feedback from the patient. Follow-up sessions after completion of the therapy allow for retrospective evaluation of change.

3.3   FEATURES OF CONTROLLED PRACTICE

Since controlled practice is not synonymous with quality assurance we will highlight some of its main elements. Controlled practice requires adherence to certain 'criteria of exactness,' which refer to the general context in which psychotherapies are planned and carried out. In the following we will propose principles and guidelines for the documentation and evaluation of therapies. Box 3.6 outlines the principles of controlled practice, which will subsequently be explained in more detail.

Box 3.6   Principles of controlled practice

1. Controlled practice is secondary to *actual therapeutic work*.
2. Controlled practice requires *structured therapy*.
3. Controlled practice is characterized by its *empirical approach* to planning, execution and evaluation of therapy.
4. Data collection follows operational *aims*, which can be used for the analysis of the therapeutic process.
5. Controlled practice demands for an integration of the therapist's and the *patient's perspectives*.
6. Analysis of empirical evidence in controlled practice is guided *by rules*.
7. Therapeutic work and single-case analysis are *documented* systematically in controlled practice.

Which perspective to take ?

Controlled practice aims at safeguarding and improving the quality of therapy. The ongoing, prospective evaluation which is part of evidence-based practice must not become an intervention in its own right if it is not intended as such. In any case, it is advisable to familiarize the client with the purpose and goal of single-case analysis. Planning the steps of therapy from the beginning may cause some therapists to feel unduly restricted in their therapeutic freedom. They may also feel pressured to justify any alternation of the therapy plan as they carry out their interventions. The patient, for instance, will gain a better understanding of his or her therapy and may view therapeutic progress as evidence of increased competence and personal control, while the therapist tests hypotheses about the effectiveness of specific interventions or therapy modules. The payer is usually most interested in evaluating the performance of the therapist; payers may be less interested in the course of therapy than in its effectiveness. Each of these diverse objectives of the different stakeholders will have to be satisfied in the interpretation of the data.

Scientific versus practical methods?

The methods used for data collection are similar to those found in clinical research; however, the context in which they are applied is different, demanding a cautious approach. The context of assessment is also different, since data collection and analysis need to be compatible with the therapeutic interventions. Planning and implementation of single-case analyses in controlled practice can only partly satisfy the full set of scientific demands. The main difference between controlled practice and clinical research lies with their respective *objectives*. Consequently, the intention is not to test scientific theories but rather to document changes that can be observed in and by the patient as a result of the therapy. Therapists develop their questions inductively, and use the single-case analysis to obtain answers. The collection of data always has to take into account the available resources in clinical practice, including limited time, material, and financial resources as well as technological equipment such as access to databases, assessment tools and data analysis tools. Since resources are limited in clinical practice, it is necessary to develop a stringent work methodology.

The 'ideal' of objective data collection faces limits in controlled practice. A particular feature of the empirical approach in evidence-based practice is the close relationship between therapist and patient, which is problematic in terms of objectivity. While a

Table 3.1 Comparison between controlled practice and clinical research

	Clinical research	Controlled practice
Legitimization	Theoretical interest	Utility/patient's well-being
Purpose/intended use	Indirect	Direct
Specific contents	E.g. finding the cause of disorders	E.g. behavior change in the patient
Origin of hypotheses	Theory (deductive)	Practice (inductive)
Formulation of hypotheses	Exact, formal	Verbal, graphical
Objectivity	Possible	Limited
Data processing	Highly technological	Adapted to practice needs
Analytical method	Statistical methods	Graphical, simple descriptive statistics
Generalizability	Possible	Primarily limited to the patient

researcher has little or no contact with subjects (in order to safeguard the objectivity of the assessment), the therapist maintains a close rapport with each patient. This relationship carries both perils and chances in terms of a practice-centered control of therapy. The close interaction between therapist and patient automatically opens up a range of information resources. At the same time the therapist has to maintain a high degree of objectivity and critical distance toward the patient. Table 3.1 summarizes the main differences between controlled practice and clinical research.

The patient perspective highlights the necessity of including the patient's view in the assessment of the therapeutic process. This also includes an appraisal of the extent to which the therapy has been concluded successfully. Consideration of the patient's perspective alongside the therapy reflects the acceptance of the patient as an equal partner throughout the therapy and documentation processes. The patient's perspective has an impact on many areas of the therapy evaluation, among them therapeutic aims, expectations, diagnostics and outcome evaluation. On the basis of the patient's aims, realistic expectations can be worked out for therapy. Scientific terms such as 'anxiety' and 'depression' must be viewed and interpreted in light of the patient's experiences. Therapists must be able to explain their understanding of these terms, and develop shared definitions with their patients. Sharing the same explanations is a step on the way toward a joint cognitive model of the problem.

A consensus with regard to therapeutic outcome between therapist and client will largely depend on the degree to which both can agree on definitions of therapeutic goals. Therapists and patients may not necessarily agree in their definition and evaluation of therapeutic goals and outcomes. The designated success of an outcome depends on the person who initially defined the criteria for outcome and on the person who decides whether these have been successfully fulfilled. Reporting on therapeutic success must state who exactly finds the therapy successful (the therapist and/or the patient).

Data collection and analysis in controlled practice are interdependent and follow explicit rules which help to maintain the greatest possible objectivity. Ideally, two independent analysts should be able to reach nearly identical conclusions provided they adhere to the same rules. Whether consequences of controlled-practice outcomes are acceptable depends largely on the degree to which rules have been followed in the analysis. Checklists that cover the entire analytical process can make evidence-based practice more efficient. They also ensure objectivity in analysis and standardized reporting, thus helping therapists to continuously improve and perfect their analytical skill. Moreover, standardized analytic strategies allow for replications. Results from similar case studies can be compared only if ways of data collection and analysis are similar; otherwise, outcomes may reflect differences in analytical strategies rather than differences resulting from therapy.

3.4 INDICATIONS FOR CONTROLLED PRACTICE

In some instances controlled practice can impede clinical practice: data collection may place a burden on patients or their social environment, or the constant focus on the current state of the problem may demotivate the patient. Controlled practice may also consume much of the therapist's time, especially during acute crisis interventions, and the collection of data should not draw too much attention away from the actual therapy. Also, since the single-case study approach relies on initially defined outcome criteria, the therapist might overlook other important changes in the patient. Conversely, data collection may become futile due to major changes in one or more areas of intervention.

Despite these eventual difficulties, clinical practice evaluation is often inevitable (see below), and controlled practice is recommended in the following situations:

1. Low motivation of patient to participate in psychotherapy
2. Concerns about exacerbation in spite of therapy/low outcome expectations
3. Expectation of liability suits on the part of the patient or his insurance company
4. Suicide risk

Controlled practice can help to identify appropriate interventions in a systematic manner, particularly in patients who repeatedly seek help from mental health services without significant improvements—so-called 'treatment failure', 'deterioration effects', 'treatment nonresponders', 'negative outcomes', 'negative effects' (Mash & Hunsley, 1993). Also, in cases where symptoms are likely to deteriorate, controlled practice can introduce an additional element of accuracy into the therapy. In the latter circumstances, indicators of success have to be adjusted accordingly. For example, during an acute crisis, a successful intervention may simply be to keep symptoms from deteriorating, and the expectation of success in terms of significant improvement seems unrealistic. While in medicine stabilizing the patient in a critical state is undeniably regarded a success, in psychotherapy unrealistic expectations frequently lead to unfavorable evaluations.

In situations where patients constitute a danger to themselves or others therapists have special responsibilities. In other situations, such as therapy involved with the panel/correctional system, it is in the public's interest that decisions about imprisonment and treatment are also based on controlled practice. Public support should also find expression in financial assistance for such efforts. Single-case evaluations can also protect psychotherapists from malpractice suits. At the very least it should be possible to provide evidence-based data about the therapeutic process. Although malpractice suits are only rarely filed due to changes in the role of the patient (from a passive recipient of health care services to an active advocate) the legitimacy of therapeutic interventions will be increasingly scrutinized.

Use of results from controlled therapies demands extra care (see Guidelines by the American Psychological Association on data protection). Although therapists may be tempted to report only selected, positive results, it is of crucial importance that results are presented in an unambiguous and complete manner. The necessity of an agreed-upon methodology for analysis and presentation of findings is at the core of controlled practice. Single-case methodology has been frequently criticized and misinterpreted throughout its long tradition, but it can be applied successfully in controlled practice.

Chapter 4

HISTORY OF THE SINGLE-CASE APPROACH

4.1 ABOUT THIS CHAPTER

This chapter provides a brief history of single-case methodology. First we will introduce some variants on single-case studies (section 4.2). We will then demonstrate how case study experiments and the use of introspection as a research method have been especially important for psychology (section 4.3). Third, we outline the varying interest in case study methodology over time (section 4.4). Finally, the significance of single-case study for research in psychotherapy is discussed (section 4.5).

4.2 VARIANTS OF SINGLE-CASE STUDY METHODOLOGY

The term 'single case' has been applied to a range of different research strategies that share one common feature: the unit of observation ($N = 1$) cannot be divided any further (see Yin, 1984). Table 4.1 lists some variants, which are arranged according to the purpose of their use into descriptive, exploratory, and explanatory approaches (see Yin, 1984).

Table 4.1   Variants of single-case studies

Descriptive	Exploratory	Explanatory
• Case study protocols or reports • Case reports • Medical records • Longitudinal studies • Biographies	• Pilot case studies • Process research • Longitudinal studies • Introspection (historical)	• Single-case experiments • Process research • Longitudinal studies

Descriptive case studies

Information is collected about individual cases; in the therapeutic context it is known as a case report. In 1895, an early document using single-case methodology was published by Freud and Breuer entitled *Studies on Hysteria*; this contained their first clinical-psychological case studies. Such clinical reports, typical for psychoanalysis at that time, recorded information on the course of individual illnesses over a period of years. The report on Anna O continues to be the best-known case report. Freud and Breuer's approach provided details on etiology and the course of various conditions.

Longitudinal analyses also have a long tradition in psychology. As early as 1882, Preyer introduced such analyses to child psychology and believed that human development during the first years of life could be followed and documented with the help of time-series designs.

In the medical field, medical records represent another variant of descriptive case studies. Medical records primarily focus on medication and treatment reports and do not usually reflect the continuous observation of patients. They frequently lack standardized ways of recording patients' responses to medication and, often, only the tolerance level for a particular medication is registered.

Exploratory case studies

Exploratory case studies help to generate hypotheses. Generally, these studies consist of very detailed documentation of individual cases—for example, on rare occasions, such as the space mission of the Russian dog Laika, enormous amounts of data were collected, since repeated missions would have been too costly. Similarly, in exceptional circumstances, such as the raising of non-human primates in human households, a vast number of observations tend to be recorded. Such situations, however, do not allow safe conclusions to be drawn, but they make it possible to reflect upon different explanations. For example, the report on the chimpanzee raised by the Kelloggs family stimulated discussions on maturation and learning (cf. Dukes, 1965). Throughout the history of psychology, individual cases have generated research in new areas. The *New York Times'* front-page coverage of the murder of Kitty Genovese inspired multiple social psychological studies on prosocial behavior, which eventually led to the birth of a new research field with social relevance ('bystander-effect', Latané & Darley, 1970).

Exploratory case studies may also include a more systematic way of collecting data. A form of exploratory case study analysis that has become known as process research contains observations on the development of communication patterns in therapies over time. Some researchers limit their use of exploratory case studies to the generation of hypotheses, while others draw on them to test specific hypotheses.

Explanatory case studies

The objective of this type of case study is to explain systematic observations. Explanation, however, places the highest demands on the way data are collected and contextual factors are controlled for, since randomization is a rare option. Great efforts are also made to rule out alternative explanations. Another difficulty of explanatory case studies is the extensive amount of data that has to be collected and the burden this may impose on the patient. On the positive side, explanatory case studies allow for the testing of models of causality, which is not immediately possible in studies where comparisons are made between two or more groups based on average values. Explanatory case studies are high on internal validity. Whereas, generalizability of case study findings to larger entities is rather limited.

Studies in which hypotheses are tested have always led to significant development in the history of medicine and psychology, especially when widely accepted 'knowledge' is disproved, as in the following examples.

In 1861, the French physician Paul Broca used case analysis to demonstrate that aphasia can be triggered by a tumor. The localization of a speech center for the first time sparked further studies in brain research. Until 1947 it was assumed that children with congenital hydrocephalus were also mentally incapacitated. A case study by Teska (1947) featuring a child with congenital hydrocephalus and an IQ of 113 led to the refutation of these views. In psychology, Watson and Rayner (1920) demonstrated that exposing an infant of several weeks to a stuffed toy rabbit could trigger a fear response after a learning period. Repeated coupling of the toy rabbit with a loud unpleasant noise eventually produced the fear response by exposure to the rabbit alone. This was explained by the principle of classical conditioning. Piaget (1952) studied the perceptual world of infants with his son Laurent as his only subject. The study established that children's perceptions are already rule-bound in the very first months of their lives. These two single-case experiments led to significant developments in psychology.

4.3 PERSONALITY DIAGNOSTICS AND CLINICAL APPROACHES

The importance of single-case methodology for personality diagnostics was recognized early by Stern (1911). He stressed the importance of an individualized psychography as a necessary addition to the nomothetical approach in psychology. In the assessment of individuality, Stern distinguished a *biographical* from a *psychographical* method. The biographical method focuses on the indivisible unity of the person. Historically, biographies occupy a central position, especially in the description of abnormality. A specific type of biography, the 'pathography'—which is also a special variant of single-case study—turns to the description of physical constitution, somatic and mental illness, hereditary conditions, paraphilia, and alcohol abuse (cf. Stern, 1911: 325).

With the help of psychography, to which Stern ascribes diagnostic potential, it is possible to describe the structure of an individual. The resulting 'psychogram' can be used to make statements about a particular person at a given point in time and about changes over long time periods. Additionally, it can be used to compare individuals with each other. It is due to Stern that the catalog of tasks within single-case diagnostics was staked out systematically at a relative early point in time. Jaspers' *Allgemeine Psychopathologie* was published almost at the same time (1913). He examined the possibilities of acquiring knowledge from an analysis of personal records (= biographics or German *Biographik*). Jaspers defined the specific sequence of biographical content in terms of a chronological pathography, and established an essential source of knowledge in psychopathology (see also von Weizäcker, 1951; Mitscherlich, 1947). The objective of pathography was to study typical patterns of progression in phasic and periodical conditions (e.g. melancholy or manic-depressive states). Within the framework of such analyses, sudden changes (e.g. growth, maturation, remission) become discernible. According to Jaspers, the onset and fading of acute periods of illness are of particular importance. In this context Jaspers (repr. 1946: 580) points out that the mathematical term 'periodicity' is not apt for such analyses, since in practice there can never be one period that matches another in any identical way; as such, neither intervals nor extent of change is comparable. However, departing somewhat from the strictest requirements, Jaspers did argue (repr. 1946: 581) that it is possible to observe periodic changes in the following three areas:

- psychopathological abnormalities (compulsive states, mood states)
- severe mood disorders (mania, melancholy)
- progressive illness processes during which periodicity develops for certain symptoms (e.g. the onset of schizophrenia, epilepsy, periodical agitation, and hallucinatory spells).

In the context of the biographical approach to change (processes, courses), Jaspers calls attention to the critical question of whether 'a singular displacement, transformation and shift of the personality brings about a new state' (p. 581) or whether the new state is caused by a continuous process. Jaspers can be credited for systematically discussing the most important features of processes involved in psychopathology, such as periodical and phasic processes.

Table 4.2   Events in the history of single-case studies

Year	Researcher	Contents	Method
1876	Wundt	General psychology	Introspection
1882	Preyer	Psychiatry	Longitudinal analyses
1885	Ebbinghaus	Cognitive research into memory/Learning curves	Self-trials
1895	Freud and Breuer	Psychoanalysis	Association and projection
1897	Stratton	Reversed retinal images	Self-tests
1911	Bleuler	Psychopathology/ Schizophrenia	Typology of individual courses of conditions
1912	Stern	Intelligence	Psychography
1913	Jaspers	General psychopathology	
1936	Piaget	Cognitive child development	Observations and experiments
1946	Cattell	Individual psychology/ Personality psychology	Intra-individual correlation; P- and O-correlation technique
1950	Zubin	Statistics	Axioms of case study statistics
1955	Kelly	Personal constructs	GRID
1961	Shapiro	Diagnostics	Personal questionnaire
1967	Chassan	Methodology	Intensive and extensive data analyses of single-case studies
1967	Eddington	Statistics	Randomized trials
1970	Box & Jenkins	Statistics	Time series analyses/ ARIMA
1975	Glass, Wilson & Gottman	Methodology	Single-case experiments and time series-based approaches

So far we have mentioned a few historical single-case studies and milestones in the development of single-case methodology. Table 4.2 contains additional publications based on single-case studies to illustrate the diversity of research in this field.

4.4   TWO HISTORICAL CASE STUDY RESEARCH METHODOLOGIES

We have previously mentioned two historical variants of single-case analysis: introspection and the single-case experiment. It is difficult to define the term 'introspection' precisely. Following Wundt (1974; see also Bretano, 1874), it is understood as a type of self-observation or inner perception during which attention is directed toward internal psychological processes and states. 'Personal self-observation', in which the researcher is his own research subject, is distinguished from 'mediated self-observation', in which a person reports self-observations to the researcher.

In the history of psychology, introspection as a method of research has been so significant that it is considered a distinctive research field today. As a method of data collection it attracted criticism because it

(a) contains risk of self-deception
(b) precludes differentiation of independent observation and actual experience (e.g. due to a lack of subject–object differentiation and the impact of the event on the observation, leading to the problem of reactivity).
(c) is limited in terms of verbal communicability and objectivity of the observer.

A crucial feature of the introspection method is its inherent subjectivity, and observations of (physical) expressions and autobiographical records have been used to supplement these 'data' as means of validation.

Addressing the relationship between experimental methodology and introspection, Wundt (1974: 2–3) wrote:

Psychological introspection goes hand in hand with the methods of experimental physiology. If one wants to put the main emphasis on the characteristic of the method, our science, experimental psychology, is to be distinguished from the ordinary mental philosophy [Seelenlehre] based purely on introspection.

The method of 'thinking aloud' used in cognitive psychology can be considered a further development of introspection. The 'thinking aloud' method requires subjects to verbalize every thought—ideally, without further reflection—while they carry out intellectual tasks. Views are divided as to whether it is possible to capture actual cognitive processes with this method. The introspection method is no longer used at present. The humanistic and the Gestalt schools of thought emphasize the subjective perspective.

Experimental methodology was introduced into psychology by physiologist Johannes Müller (1942). Physiology was then a principal scientific discipline, and it served as an important source in the development of psychology. Renowned scientists such as Hermann Helmholtz were among the proponents of experimental methodology. Wilhelm Wundt contributed to the dissemination of the experimental method, and two of his students, Edward Bradford Titchener and William James, introduced it to the United States. Wundt, however, was critical regarding the scope and applicability of experimentation. He believed that the power of experiments to produce evidence was limited to lower mental processes, and viewed introspection as the more appropriate method for higher mental processes. Danziger (1990: 207, n. 22) wrote of Wundt:

> I speak of the hopes of the young Wundt advisedly because in due course he lost the enthusiasm for the possibilities of the experimental method in psychology that he had expressed in his first major publication.

Although, there was a reluctance to fully embrace experimentation as a valid method of psychological research, Ebbinghaus, who carried out a number of experimental self-tests, laid out the foundation for a psychology of memory. But even Ebbinghaus (1885), in the preface to his monograph *Über das Gedächtnis* (Engl. *Memory*,

1913), stated a number of concerns that continue to be of relevance to case study methodology today. He intended to give his results a greater general validity by carrying out the same memory experiments (the memorization of meaningless syllables) on himself during two time periods, in 1879/80 and 1883/84. The stretch of three years between the two experiments allowed him to *replicate* the results of 1879/80 while controlling for memory bias and other effects.

4.5   DISPLACEMENT OF THE SINGLE-CASE APPROACH BY QUESTIONNAIRES

We now need to ask how the single-case method lost so much of its influence, for its initial dominance at the turn of the 20th century gradually disappeared. This is clearly illustrated by the declining proportion of articles published in the *American Journal of Psychology* involving single-case studies (see Figure 4.1). Other journals, such as the *Journal of Experimental Psychology*, show a similar trend.

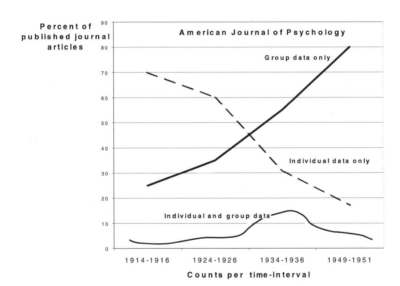

Figure 4.1   Decline in publication of single-case studies in the *American Journal of Psychology* (data from Danziger, 1990)

This development can be explained, at least in part, by 'Zeitgeist' and contextual factors (Danziger, 1990; Boring, 1929). As a new discipline, psychology felt pressure from established fields such as medicine, physics, and biology. 'Soft' research methods like intro-spection did little to improve its status, while the introduction of experimental methods helped it to gain acceptance from the scien-tific community. Thus, remodeled after the natural sciences, the objective of psychology became to find rules of universal validity. Idiographical analyses were discarded as unscientific and intuitive—a criticism that was even brought forward in the field of mental health (Warnock, Mintz & Twemlow, 1979; Campbell & Stanley, 1963).

In addition to experiments, questionnaires soon became a popular method of data collection. Quetelet (1835) was a pioneer in the development of questionnaire design. Surveys in the social sciences were conducted as early as the 1860s in Berlin (see Bem, Rappard & van Hoorn, 1984). In comparison to experiments and introspection, questionnaires were a fast and economic way of collecting a great amount of data. They made population, or 'mass', data accessible. The use of questionnaires by renowned scientists raised the acceptance of this method, as Danziger (1990: 75) has shown:

> Charles Darwin used it in his study of emotional expression, and his cousin, Francis Galton, used it in his study of heredity and mental imagery. Such usage helped to strengthen the legitimacy of statisti-cal data compiled on the basis of questionnaires as a source of scientific knowledge.

The questionnaire method helped to answer important, primarily psychodiagnostic questions. It was used, for example, to select individuals for military service and to screen applicants regarding their suitability for jobs in industry. Questionnaires were also used to study the causes of various forms of criminal behavior. Questionnaire data gathered from representative samples allowed researchers to reach a new set of conclusions. Any statement made by an individual could now be compared to a referential popu-lation. This meant that variability in terms of differences from average population values became discernible. It was the golden age of dimensional personality concepts (Guilford, 1940; Cattell, 1944; Eysenck, 1944, 1953).

Quetelet understood that 'fictitious' average values must not be applied to individual cases. This limiting factor of the questionnaire method was politely ignored in the face of the advantages the method seemed to offer. Group-oriented studies that used questionnaires became the dominant approach in research in the social sciences. Danziger (1990) labeled this development as 'the triumph of the aggregate'. A very important contribution in defense of the single-case approach in clinical psychology was made by Zubin (1950) in the 'Symposium on Statistics for the Clinician'. At a time when single-case studies were unpopular in psychology, Zubin (1950: 1) characterized the situation as follows:

> Present day statistical treatment of clinical data is primarily group-centered rather than individual-centered. [. . .] The clinician on his part has begun to feel the need for objectifying some of his empirically gained intuitions, and the statistician on his part has begun to wonder whether his present day tools are adequate to handle the complexity of the clinical case.

New axioms were needed to guide the analysis of individual cases (see Box 4.1).

As a consequence of Zubin's fundamental work, the single-case methodology experienced a renaissance. Critics such as Campbell and Stanley (1963), however, found little to commend in single-case studies: 'Such studies have such a total absence of control as to be of almost no scientific value' (p. 6). They later revised this view (see Hilliard, 1993) and even wrote the preface to Yin's (1989) work on the single-case methodology. Advances in statistics, such as the use of a single-factorial analysis of variance in case studies (Shine & Bower, 1971), and in diagnostics, with individualized questionnaires (Shapiro, 1961), and the increasing demand for quality assurance cleared the way for the introduction of monitoring and documentation techniques for clinical practice, such as the technique of controlled practice. Nonetheless, some of the classical problems concerning the measurement of change (Harris, 1963) remain unresolved today (Cronbach & Furby, 1970; Krauth, 1990).

Box 4.1   Axioms of single-case research by Zubin (1950)

1. In the study of a single individual, especially of a so-called abnormal individual, we must treat each case as an independent universe. Later when the characteristics of each of these universes become known, we may be able to classify them into groups of like-structured or similar universes. Until such knowledge becomes available, it is unwarranted to classify individuals as equivalent, even if they have identical scores on a series of tests.
2. Every individual is characterized by a given level of performance, of which the observed test score is a random sample.
3. Every individual is also characterized by a given degree of variability around the level of performance . . . The behavioral field as well as the internal environment of the individual is subject to the influence of slight alternations in the stimulation of the organism internally or externally, to which it responds with changes in performance, but these changes in performances follow a characteristic pattern dependent upon the individual's characteristic variability or homeostatic pattern.
4. The effect of change in stimulation, internal and external, is to bring about an alternation in either the level of performance, the variation in performance, or both.

Kiresuk and Sherman (1968) have criticized the use of standardized, global measures that followed the nomothetic principle with the words '. . . there has been a tendency to use a fixed battery of evaluation measures regardless of the individual patient characteristics or problems' (p. 444). This statement ignores the fact that individualized approaches in the form of 'personal questionnaires' already existed (pioneer work conducted by Shapiro, 1961).

4.6 SINGLE-CASE AND PSYCHOTHERAPY RESEARCH

The history of psychotherapy research illustrates the renaissance of the single-case method and the change in research questions it

Box 4.2   Therapy Session Report (Patient Form, from Orlinsky & Howard, 1975)

1. How do you feel about the therapy session that you have just completed?
2. What did you talk about during this session?
3. What did you want or hope to get out of this therapy session?
4. How did you act toward your therapist during this session?
5. How did you feel during this session?
6. To what extent were you looking forward to coming to this session?
7. How freely were you able to talk with your therapist during this session?
8. How clearly did you know what you wanted to talk about during this session?
9. How well did your therapist seem to understand how you were feeling and what was really on your mind during this session?
10. Do you feel that what your therapist said and did during this session was helpful to you?
11. Do you feel that you made progress in this session in dealing with the problems for which you are in therapy?
12. How well do you feel that you are getting along, emotionally and psychologically, at this time?
13. What do you feel that you got out of this session?
14. To what extent are you looking forward to your next session?
15. How did your therapist act toward you during this session?
16. How did your therapist seem to feel during this session?

entailed. Psychotherapy research also points out the necessity of quality control and controlled-practice measures. In the 1960s, forms of psychotherapy such as behavior therapy and client-centered therapy were established alongside psychoanalysis. At the beginning of the first period (see the periods of research in psychotherapy as defined by Shapiro), the principal question was whether psychological therapies produced beneficial outcomes at all. Eysenck (1952) triggered the discussion with his widely received study on the effectiveness of psychoanalytic treatment of neuroses. At that time group designs were the preferred method of research, and single-case studies were of marginal importance. Psychotherapists managed to establish their therapies alongside medication and technology-based treatments.

During the second phase of psychotherapy research, the focus shifted toward studying patient and therapist characteristics. The goal was to accomplish a perfect 'match' between patients and thera-pists and to identify differential treatment indications (Berzins, 1977; Luborsky, Crits-Christoph & Auerbach, 1988). A wide range of per-sonality traits was considered on both sides (Karasu, 1986). This research strategy, however, did not produce a profound understand-ing of what the actual mechanisms were that brought about changes in the patient. Thus, the third phase of psychotherapy research cen-tered on microanalysis. Treatment sessions were scrutinized with the highest degree of methodological sensitivity to identify the crucial moments in a session that may have effected the changes observed in the patient. The 'Therapy Session Report' in Box 4.2 is an example of an analysis of the microdynamics of therapy ('Patient Form' by Orlinsky & Howard, 1975).

In conclusion, research methods in psychotherapy research have shifted from outcome to process measures, eventually leading to a revival of single-case approaches.

The overall influence of psychotherapy research on clinical prac-tice has nevertheless remained limited. 'At present, clinical re-search has little or no influence on clinical practice' (see Barlow, 1981: 147, as well as Garfield 1982 and Smith, Glass & Miller, 1980).

Today we can discern a fourth period of psychotherapy research (Linden, 1987): practice-oriented research. This type of research seeks to answer such questions as: 'What results do therapies produce in the natural environment?' An early example in the pharmacological sector is the Private Practice Group of Philadelphia (Rickels & Hesbacher, 1969). Thus, controlled practice can be viewed as a practice-integrated strategy of psychotherapy research if data from single-case analyses are evaluated.

Chapter 5

ILLUSTRATING THE STEPS OF CONTROLLED PRACTICE

5.1 ABOUT THIS CHAPTER

This chapter illustrates the concrete tasks therapists must accomplish in controlled practice. The procedure described in Chapter 3 will be explained with the help of an example and a typical plan of action. While other chapters provide more thorough analyses, as indicated in Table 5.1, the goal of this chapter is to give a general introduction of controlled practice.

Additional tasks listed in Table 5.1 can be easily integrated into therapy. They add further clarity to the steps of action taken by the therapist. Of these tasks, only data collection and analysis require specific skills. In the following sections we will describe these tasks in greater detail.

5.2 STEP 1: GAINING INFORMED CONSENT

Patients must be asked to give their informed consent to both collection and analysis of data as part of the contractual agreement with the therapist. Therapists also need to obtain permissions

Table 5.1   Tasks in controlled practice

Therapy tasks	Tasks of clinical practice	Chapter
Step 1. Write therapy contract	Gain informed consent	
Step 2. Analyze problem	Graphical problem description	Chapter 6
Step 3. Plan therapy	Graphical treatment explanation	Chapter 7
Step 4. Plan therapy	Develop a questionnaire	Chapter 8
Step 5. Analyze goal	Patient's expectations	Chapter 8
Step 6. Plan therapy	Therapist's expectations	Chapter 9
Step 7. Carry out intervention	Data collections	Chapter 9
Step 8. Complete therapy	Data analysis	Chapter 10
Step 9. Describe case	Document	Chapter 11

regarding the further use of data. The questions shown in Box 5.1 indicate elements that should be included in an informed consent sheet.

Box 5.1   Details of the Informed Consent Form.

(1) I have received information about the content and process of single-case analysis.

(2) I agree to the collection of data as part of controlled practice. I understand that at any point in time I can revoke this decision regardless of prior consent.

(3) I have been informed of the intent to use the collected data in the following way(s):

. . . .

. . . .

. . . .

(4) It may become necessary that my therapist has to compromise my confidentiality to protect my safety and/or that of other parties. In these situation my therapist will, as part of my treatment, consult with other professionals. In this event, I shall release my therapist from the confidentiality agreement and consent to the sharing of information with other professionals

. . . .

. . . .

(5) I have been informed of all foreseeable inconveniences and additional burden arising from the single-case evaluation.

_____   _____
Patient's signature   *Therapist's signature*

Place / Date: Place / Date:

5.3   STEP 2: A GRAPHICAL PROBLEM DESCRIPTION

Having ascertained the patient's consent to therapy and evaluation, the therapist engages in problem analysis by collecting all information necessary to gain insight in the problem and its crucial aspects. A 'graphical problem description' (see Box 5.2; see also Chapter 7) can help to structure this information.

Box 5.2   A graphical problem description

A graphical problem description is a graphical summary of major problems, including possible causes and maintaining factors.

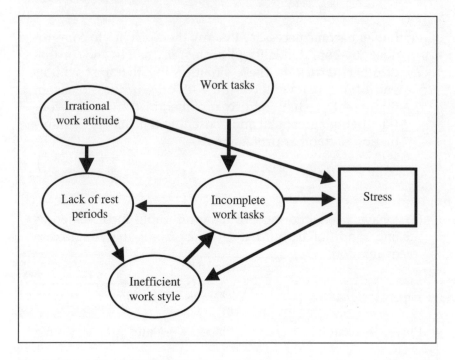

Figure 5.1 Graphical problem description. (Causes and influencing factors are presented in ovals, symptoms in squares)

The graphical problem description complements case history and problem analysis. We will use the following case description to construct a graphical problem description.

Excerpts from a written case description

The patient reports that he has been suffering from chronic occupational strain for the last eight months. Because of high work demands he is not able to take any breaks. An attempt to reduce his workload failed due to a lack of cooperation on the part of his supervisor. The combination of limited productivity and increasing work demands is causing such a degree of stress that any work becomes impossible at times. Current workplace situation is not conducive to a change of the patient's problem. As the problem becomes more evident, the patient fears losing his job. Since none of his earlier attempts to solve the problem has yet succeeded, the patient has decided to seek professional help from a psychotherapist.

After the patient has explained the nature of the problem, therapist and patient create a 'graphical problem description' that summarizes essential information concisely and clearly. Figure 5.1 illustrates the problem description and organizes the explanations developed cooperatively by the therapist and the patient. The patient's irrational attitude toward work (demand: 'The work must always be done immediately and flawlessly') has been identified as the main reason or 'cause' for the current stress experience. The amount of work is the consequence of the patient's inefficient work style (deficient problem-solving skills) and his lack of assertiveness when requesting a more reasonable amount of work from the supervisor. The absence of rest periods results from this irrational work attitude and the accumulation of unfinished work.

5.4 STEP 3: A GRAPHICAL TREATMENT EXPLANATION

The patient's goals determine all treatment planning. In our example, the following goals may be identified:

- Stress reduction
- Acceptance of being 'not perfect' (realistic work attitude)
- Reduction of work load
- Ability to relax and take breaks

The therapist recommends the following *intervention strategies* to meet these goals:

- Discussion with the patient of his working style with the aim of cognitive restructuring (Ellis, 1973)
- Progressive muscle relaxation (Jacobson, 1938)
- Assertiveness training (Hollins & Trower, 1986)
- Self-instructions to improve problem-solving skills (Meichenbaum, 1977)

This list gives only a rough indication of what the therapy might consist of, and it remains unclear which aims these interventions

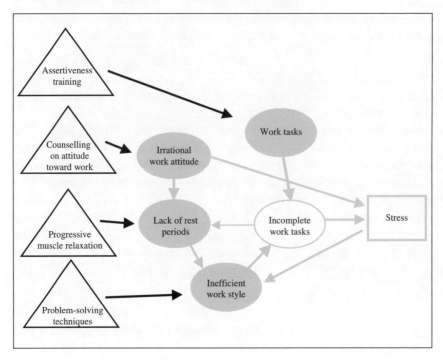

Figure 5.2 Therapeutic goals and intervention techniques. (Triangles show intervention strategies, shaded ovals show intervention aims, transparent ovals contain conditions, and squares contain symptoms)

pursue. The 'graphical treatment explanation' combines intervention strategies to their intended effects (see Figure 5.2). The therapist begins with a description of the aims of intervention, depicted in Figure 5.2 in gray shaded ovals. The intervention strategies are then added (in triangles) and connected by arrows to the problem (square).

Additional interventions may be added if selected strategies prove unsuccessful or insufficient in bringing about the intended changes. For example, nonspecific relaxation techniques may be replaced by a specific stress management program. Such modifications of therapy may be added later to the graphical treatment explanation.

After concluding the planning of the therapy, therapist and patient need to develop a problem-focused therapy process questionnaire. Throughout the therapy the patient will be asked to rate and describe changes.

5.5   STEP 4: DEVELOP A THERAPY PROCESS QUESTIONNAIRE

The process questionnaire assesses relevant changes resulting from the therapeutic intervention. It also provides information on whether the skills emphasized in therapy are actually used by the patient in daily life. The graphical treatment explanation guides therapist and patient in identifying specific questions.

Contents

Clearly, it is necessary to check whether or not recently acquired skills (relaxation exercises and problem-solving) prove useful. Perceived stress is the primary symptom targeted for modification through a diverse set of interventions (global effect). Apart from global effects two additional outcomes of the intervention will be tested. First: To what extent is the patient able to set limits in the amount of work he receives? (effect of the assertiveness training). Second: Has the attitude toward work changed as a result of the discussions on the patient's irrational belief system?

Operationalization

Questions should be formulated as concisely as possible. In our example (Figure 5.3), perceived stress is the core outcome measure (Question 1). The patient's satisfaction with accomplished work tasks is used as an indicator of changes in his attitude toward work (labeled 'Satisfaction with work', Question 2). Daily self-assessments show whether the amount of work has actually decreased (Question 3). The number of relaxation exercises carried out on each work day indicates the degree of relaxation that has really become part of the patient's daily routines (Question 4). Problem-solving skills are also assessed in terms of how often these strategies are used (Question 5). Figure 5.3 illustrates the relationship between the therapy process questionnaire and the graphical treatment explanation. In our example the process questionnaire comprises the five questions shown in Figure 5.4)

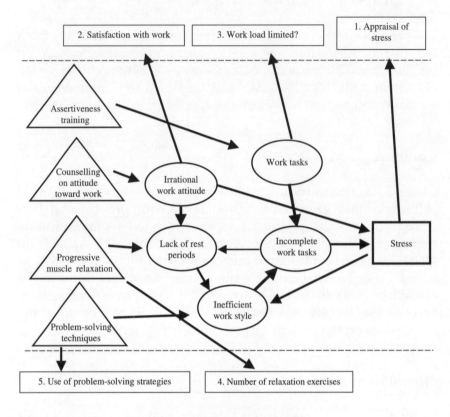

Using recently acquired skills

Figure 5.3   Relationship between therapy process questionnaire and graphical treatment explanation

5.6   STEP 5: PATIENT'S EXPECTATIONS

The patient's expectations of therapy need to be clarified. Patients are asked to appraise their current situation (Actual Condition, AC) and to indicate the extent of change they expect as a result of the therapy (Specified Condition, SC). This approach to define clear goals will facilitate the outcome analysis. Both actual and specified condition are listed in separate questionnaires (see Figure 5.5).

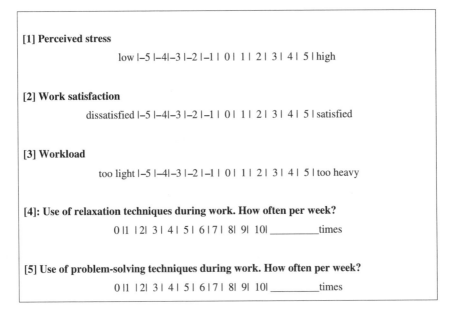

Figure 5.4   Example of a process questionnaire

5.7   STEP 6: THERAPIST'S EXPECTATIONS

The therapist expects the patient to apply the cognitive and behavioral strategies taught during the course of therapy, and, as a
consequence, positive outcomes should become evident (effect
evaluation). These expectations are discussed in greater detail in
Chapter 7, 'A graphical treatment explanation'. The diagram already displays connections between intervention strategies and
outcome variables. At this point we will examine more closely the
variability in outcome variables throughout therapy. The therapist
inserts his expectations about the prospective changes in outcome
variables into the evaluation diagram (see Figure 5.6). Later, these
expectations can be compared with empirical data and feedback
provided by the patient.

Perceived stress, as the principal symptom, is expected to decrease
gradually as a result of increased satisfaction with work (1st transfer effect) and of reduction in the work load (2nd transfer effect).
Improved work satisfaction reflects a change in attitude toward

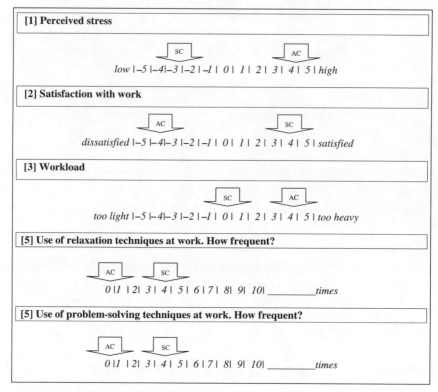

Figure 5.5   Examples of the patient regarding therapy

work, and the enhanced work efficiency can be attributed to the use of problem-solving skills. Relaxation exercises also boost work productivity (see Figure 5.6).

5.8   STEP 7: DATA COLLECTION

Next, data collection details must be addressed. Most importantly, a decision has to be made about how often the therapy process questionnaire needs to be completed. In our example changes taking place during working hours are most relevant; thus the patient is asked to fill in the questionnaire at the end of each working day. Completed questionnaires are passed on to the therapist and are jointly analyzed by the therapist and the patient at the beginning of each session. It is important that the therapist sets aside enough time to analyze the daily protocols in order to:

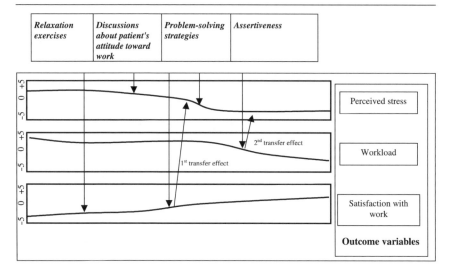

Figure 5.6 Therapist's expectations

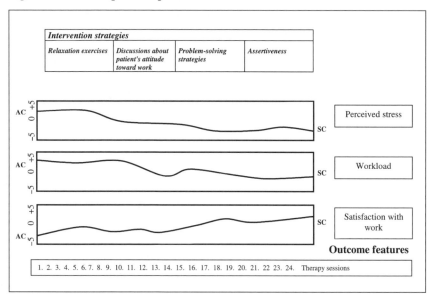

Figure 5.7 Process diagram

- address effectively the everyday experiences of the patient during therapy
- differentially reinforce the outcomes from self-observations
- give adequate support to the patient's self-management.

Patients should be trained to keep a diary. A dry run of entering daily information into a questionnaire will allow the patient to clarify open questions about the procedure and possibly provide additional information on the actual condition (AC).

5.9   STEP 8: DATA ANALYSIS

Data analysis concludes the evaluation at the end of therapy. The therapist can illustrate the changes in the outcome variables graphically (see Figure 5.7). The variability in outcomes over time is shown along a scale indicating the number of therapy sessions. In the following we will focus on two particular aspects of the analysis:

- Patient's appraisal of the therapeutic outcomes
- Examination of the working theory postulated by the therapist.

Therapy success

The patient's outcome expectations are compared (Specified Condition; see Figure 5.5) with actual outcomes at the end of therapy (beginning with session 18) using a process diagram (Figure 5.7). A visual inspection shows that all the goals have been accomplished. Graphically illustrated changes are consistent with the patient's verbal reports. The patient describes how he has learned 'to take breaks', and how this has positively affected his non-work behavior (an area that has not been systematically assessed). This is additionally validated by reports of the patient. Changes achieved in all three outcome measures are also *statistically significant* (test on positive trends and goal attainment). Whether the specified condition (SC) is met may be verified with the help of additional statistical tests. The therapy has succeeded in bringing about the desired changes in the patient. Outcomes also appear to be sufficiently persistent in time.

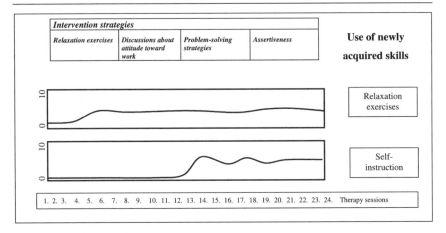

Figure 5.8 Examining the use of newly acquired skills

Working theory

To examine whether the therapy has worked, it has to be demonstrated that the patient actually uses the new skills in daily life. Figure 5.8, which illustrates the use of new skills in the patient's working day, clearly indicates that the patient has developed new skills during therapy. Progressive muscle relaxation is the strategy the patient adopted first in his daily life (from the 6th session onward, approximately four times a day). From the 14th session he used problem-solving strategies (on average five times daily). These skills seem to have been firmly implemented in the patient's everyday life, and outcome are attributed to the regular use of this set of new skills (see Figure 5.8). These findings support the therapist's hypotheses and support the use of selected intervention in similar cases.

5.10   STEP 9: DOCUMENTATION

In order to document both therapy and evaluation, results from each step are combined by archiving the following information:

1. Graphical problem description
2. Graphical treatment explanation

3. Therapy process questionnaire
4. Patient's expectations (Actual Condition vs Specified Condition)
5. Therapist's expectations (Evaluation diagram)
6. Use of newly acquired skills
7. Intervention effects (Process diagram)
8. Data description (How many assessments? Who is responsible for coding the responses?)
9. Statistical findings
10. Additional comments by the therapist

These sets of information constitute an intrinsic part of every single-case analysis; thus documentation is more or less synonymous with archiving the information gathered throughout the therapy. These therapy documents can be used later for a variety of purposes—for example, in professional dialogue with other therapists, given the patient's consent. The specific therapy can also be reconstructed and reanalyzed on the basis of these documents.

Chapter 6

DIAGNOSTICS: A GRAPHICAL PROBLEM DESCRIPTION

6.1 ABOUT THIS CHAPTER

This chapter addresses the development of a 'graphical problem description': a tool designed to help therapists to summarize their patients' problems in a clear and concise way. A graphical problem description should comprise only the most pertinent information such as biographical conditions, current social environment or recent coping attempts. Its objective is to provide the therapist with an easily-accessible display of patients' current situations as well as the hypothesized causes. Subsequent steps in controlled practice will build upon this procedure, for instance, an explanation of proposed treatment (see Chapter 7) and a process questionnaire (see Chapter 8).

6.2 CONTENT OF THE GRAPHICAL PROBLEM DESCRIPTION

Since every problem situation is defined by certain unique features, a problem description solely based on a psychiatric classification (Box 6.1) cannot be exhaustive. Psychological disorders of the same category are known to show great variability between

---

Box 6.1   Psychiatric classification

A nosology is a classification system describing well-known disorders and associated symptoms in precise terms. The most widely used classifications are the American Psychiatric Association's DSM-IV (Diagnostic and Statistical Manual, 4th revision) and the ICD-10 (International Classification of Disease, 10th revision) of the World Health Organization. Both systems assign unique codes to symptoms and behaviors that are characteristic of a specific disorder.

---

individuals—a fact that must not be ignored when planning the treatment (Haynes, 1998).

Difficulties arise in cases where therapists must integrate and present findings from a variety of data sources in a way that is still understandable to their patients. Therapists may also wish to use specific diagnostic information to prepare for interventions. A graphical problem description can facilitate these tasks. The following core questions may help to structure the task of creating a thorough description:

- In what areas does the patient feel limited in his or her activities (symptoms)?
- How do different problems interrelate?
- What factors supposedly cause, trigger, and maintain the symptoms (causality analysis)?
- Which factors lend themselves to therapeutic intervention?

A well-tested analytical approach known as functional analysis (Box 6.2) enables a concrete, situation-specific description of a particular problem to be given.

A behavioral functional analysis can be carried out either for an individual (individual or idiosyncratic approach) or for a particular clinical condition (general or nomothetic approach). A therapist can use this general functional analysis for an individual case as a guideline. Box 6.3 lists a few examples of disorders to which

---

Box 6.2   Functional analysis

Functional analysis is a model based on psychological learning theory in which information on the causes of problem behaviors and their maintaining factors is arranged in a systematic way. It is a method of organizing clinical findings, also known as SORKC-model (Kanfer & Saslow, 1969). The acronym SORKC pertains to a kind of 'behavior equation' consisting of the following components:

S = Stimuli
O = Organism variables
R = Behavioral response
K = Consequences
C = Contingencies

Box 6.3   Examples of applied functional analysis

Noncompliance in chronic illness	Vandereycken & Meermann (1988)
Delinquency	Jones & Heskins (1988)
Depression	Dougher & Hackbert (1994)
Developmental disabilities	Bijou & Dunitz-Johnson (1981)
Reluctant speech	Mace & West (1986)
School refusal	Kearney & Silverman (1990)
Self-injury	Iwata et al. (1993)
Social skills	Hughes & Sullivan (1988)
Anorexia nervosa and bulimia nervosa	Slade (1982)

---

functional analysis has been applied. It is the therapist's task to adapt this general scheme to the individual case in a therapy.

Functional analysis results in a complex structure comprising behaviors, situational characteristics, and mental processes, and a graphical problem description is used to summarize this information. 'Clinical theory' (Bruch, 1998) supplies sound theoretical grounds for this integration. It is based on a 'case formulation model' which was first described by Meyer (1957) and further developed at the University College London (UCL) by Meyer and Turkat (1979). While the UCL team primarily pursued the goal of giving therapy a solid theoretical foundation, we have aimed solely at presenting problems of the clinical situation prior to the therapy.

Prior to beneficial use of a graphical problem description some basic rules need to be understood. One of the most pertinent issues that therapists need to clarify is their understanding of causality. In the following section we will introduce several concepts of causality and finally give a description of contemporary causality concepts related to the functional analysis approach (Haynes, 1998).

6.3   CLINICAL EXPLANATIONS OF PATIENT BEHAVIOR

It is human nature to seek to uncover the meaning of, or the purpose behind, our behavior in everyday life. Facing diseases or personal conflicts, we readily ask what led to their emergence, and our reasoning quickly extends to identifying personal responsibility (e.g. guilt) and personal significance for the patient. Since attribution of causality is often biased by a flawed psychological process, we will examine it more closely.

Reported loneliness and problems with sleep may be due to a marital crisis, but any number of alternative explanations could be responsible. The reason for flawed explanations lies with the specific way in which information in a given situation is being processed. Psychology has shown that perception, memory, and conclusions are subject to systematic errors (Galotti, 1999). All evaluations are based on perceptions, which may be highly selective because of our deficiency to process and account for all available information (errors of information reception). Sometimes new information is added without our being aware of it (errors of information storage), and even if we succeed in integrating all essentials, we might not necessarily be able to remember them properly (errors of information recollection). For example, we may make connections between events where none exists. When a door slams and a light turns off at the same time, we might assume a causal link due to the temporal occurrence of events (phenomenological causality; Duncker, 1935). Particularly, events which are temporally connected and appear only rarely are certain to evoke causal interpretations (Michotte, 1963). In a clinical context, associations between critical life events (first rare event) and current symptoms (second rare event) may become pervasive. However, little is known about mediating perceptions and attitudes that may link a traumatic experience to clinical symptoms.

Apart from these errors of information processing, external circumstances are of crucial importance. For example, the amount of available information during the first therapist–patient contact may seriously influence our explanation of psychological disorders. A lack of information may result in prioritizing certain relationships as causal, and the role of the actor is supposedly overestimated. On the contrary, when comprehensive information is available, more detailed analyses can be carried out according to the 'covariance principle' (Kelley, 1973). Several therapeutic approaches direct attention to the prototypical causes of psychological problems, such as the failure to successfully complete developmental phases, or misguided cognitive appraisals. Different schools of therapy focus on different theoretical aspects, leading therapists to evaluate their observations in a way that is consistent with given theory. The results of attribution research (e.g. 'internal/external control', Rotter, 1954; 'personal construct', Kelly, 1955, 1958) are therefore of special significance for any clinical theory. This brief presentation shows that both therapist and patient should consider all explanations as preliminary and subject to continuous revision. Feelings of guilt (Hart & Honoré, 1973) in the patient may indicate monocausal and person-centered attributions (fundamental attributional error), and it may be of interest to note that the Greek word for 'cause' is a synonym for 'blame' and 'accusation' (Eimer, 1987). Therapists might offer alternative explanatory concepts which emphasize, for example, the importance of situational impacts, learning processes, and personal attitudes or perceptions.

6.4   CONCEPTS OF CAUSALITY AND THE EXPLANATION OF PSYCHOLOGICAL DISORDERS

The classic concept of 'causality' has a long history in philosophy and scientific theory. We will begin with simple concepts of causality, then introduce more complex concepts and apply these to the explanation of psychological disorders. In Chapter 8 we will illustrate the role of causal explanations in treatment decisions.

The most widely known concept of causality was developed by Hume in 1740. He postulated three attributes of causal relationships:

(a) proximity in time and in space of cause and effect
(b) precedence of cause
(c) consistency in the relation of cause and effect

Hume's concept is *monocausal* and does not address the problem of alternative explanations. When environmental factors fail to be constant, more complex concepts of causality apply. Figure 6.1 illustrates Hume's unidirectional causality concept.

We will now apply principle 1 to the explanation of a social phobia. A patient reports that a situation (stimulus A, a crowd) leads to a

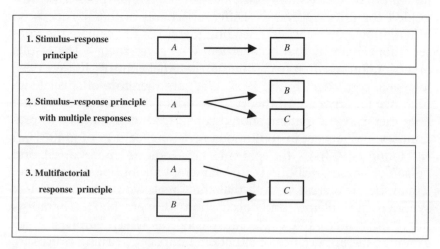

Figure 6.1   Direct causal relationships

behavior (response B, fear). Such coincidence of situational impact and behavior is known as the *stimulus–response principle*. Since several symptoms may be observed in the patient, however, principle 2 better captures the observation (fear and nausea). Because most psychological disorders are diverse in appearance, therapists are more likely to apply the second variant. This principle is known as *stimulus–response with multiple responses*. In some cases, several conditions have to coincide before a response is triggered in the patient. In our example of social phobia, several conditions (a crowd, an enclosed room) may trigger the fear response. This situation is known as the *multifactorial response principle*. In this view, the response simply constitutes the end of the process, without any further consequences. In the example of social phobia, the fact that one might remember similar situations could be introduced as a mediating link between stimulus and response. This connection of causality is known as *stimulus–response–chain principle* (see Figure 6.2).

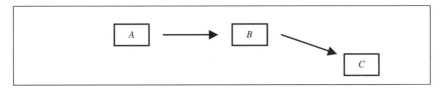

Figure 6.2   Stimulus–response chain principle

All previously described principles have been unidirectional, that is, responses did not retroactively affect their causes. However, several theories in the therapeutical context do postulate some interdependence of factors. For example, people's relationship on the behavioral level could be analyzed in terms of interactive processes (Beach, Sandeen & O'Leary, 1990; Hazelett & Haynes, 1992). This leads to another principle, the *stimulus–response feedback* illustrated in Figure 6.3.

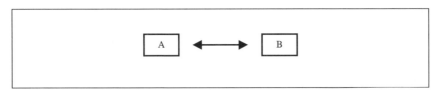

Figure 6.3   Stimulus–response feedback principle

Still another multidirectional type of causality is present when a 'cause' exerts an influence on itself (without the involvement of a second variable). For example, vegetative symptoms, such as heart palpitations, may trigger anxiety and in turn set off further vegetative responses. This is known as *recursive dependency*. Mood states can also become self-sustaining, for example when during a gloomy state of mind more negative memories are generated and current events are perceived as distressing in consequence (Beck, 1976).

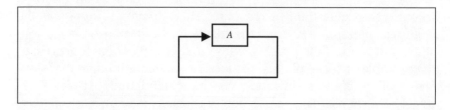

Figure 6.4   Recursive dependency principle

All these concepts of causality have been deterministic; that is, for any given stimulus A, response B must follow. However, conditions are still idealized, excluding other possible influences and explanations. But human behavior takes place in complex conditions, and thus can be predicted only within a certain range of probability. As a consequence, probabilistic approaches are at the heart of psychology. In conjectures like 'when A is present, then the likelihood for the occurrence of B is higher', different consequences can be assigned different weights. The therapist can then focus on a few selected relationships and intervene only in these areas. This weighting of strong and weak relationships can be illustrated graphically by varying the line width of arrows that indicate the effects between variables. Different concepts of causality may be combined and graphically presented in a graphical problem description. In 1975, Sameroff and Chandler described psychological disorders with the help of different causality concepts. They distinguished three main variants of multiple causality: the main effect model, the interactive model, and the transactional model (Box 6.4).

The most recent contributions relating causality concepts to clinical disorders are due to the work of Haynes (Haynes, 1998; Haynes,

---

Box 6.4   Multifactorial effect models by Sameroff and Chandler (1975)

The *main effect model* is based on a necessary but not sufficient condition that generates the symptoms. This model is applied to mental disorders due to medical conditions, i.e. Down's Syndrome.

The *interactive model* incorporates several aspects of multifactorial response principle. It is different from the main effect model in that several independent factors are viewed as having equal impacts on the psychological disorder. An example is the diathesis-stress model.

The *transactional model* postulates a feedback loop connecting the effect and the cause. This model is well-suited to describe person–environment relationships, such as situations in which patients' disorders have a systematic effect on the people in their environment, thereby reinforcing, attenuating, or stabilizing the disorders.

Leisen & Blaine, 1997; Haynes, Spain & Oliveira, 1993). Haynes's view of causality is combined with functional analysis leading to what he calls 'functional analytic clinical case model' (FACCM – 1997) or 'functional analytic causal model' (FACM – 1998). Although very formal in notation, this model lends itself quite easily to graphic representation by providing an adequate template (Haynes & O'Brian, 1990; see Figure 6.5).

Figure 6.5 relates symptoms of a patient to his or her presumed underlying causes and thus illustrates the information gathered in the diagnostic process. Haynes gives the following rules for interpreting the graph, which we adhere to later:

1. The line width of arrows symbolizes the strength of a relationship.
2. Every element belongs to a distinctive class:

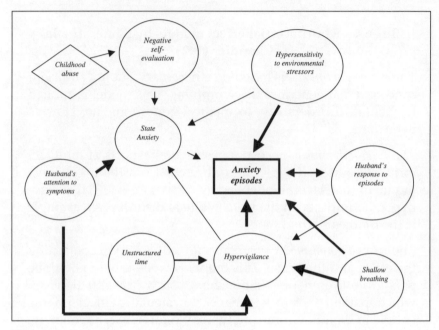

Legend:

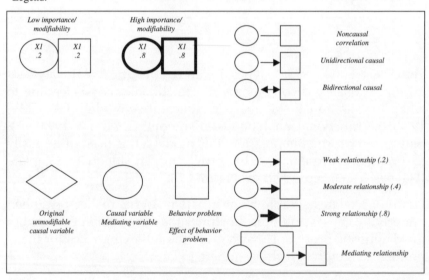

Figure 6.5 Functional analytic causal model (FACM) (cf. Haynes, 1998, p. 32)

(a) the diamond ($\Diamond$) symbolizes the causes of a disorder that cannot be changed, for example, previous events leading to post-traumatic stress;

(b) the oval ($\bigcirc$) symbolizes conditions or states that trigger and maintain behavior; an example is the response of a spouse to an anxiety episode;

(c) the square ($\square$) symbolizes the behavior (e.g. anxiety episodes) to which causal arrows point.

As mentioned previously, it is possible to integrate the notion of causality by Haynes, Spain and Oliveira (1993) with functional analysis when, in addition to the requirement of simple covariation, some further conditions are met: (a) the causal variable reliably precedes its effect; (b) there is a logical mechanism for the causal relationship; and (c) alternative explanations for the observed covariance can be reasonably excluded. The following aspects then become important for controlled practice:

1. FACCM allows for a hypothetical case formulation. Actual presentation is considered preliminary and subject to revision on the basis of new evidence.
2. A dynamic case formulation is possible, enabling statements about the sequence in time and the development of symptoms.
3. The FACCM is probabilistic.
4. The FACCM encompasses both unidirectional and bidirectional relationships.
5. The FACCM can attain different degrees of specificity and includes moderating variables.

6.5   DEVELOPMENT OF A GRAPHICAL PROBLEM DESCRIPTION

For the graphical representation of diagnostic information, Haynes's approach needs to be modified in order to 'fit' into a therapeutic frame of reference and to meet the requirements of the current single-case analysis. On the one hand, it is important that the collection of information is precise and complete; on the other, it needs to remain comprehensible. It is clear that any additional burden imposed on the patient and/or the therapist by the collection of data must be as minimal as possible. The diagram should include only a few central elements, intervention techniques will be added to the graph at a later stage. The graphical problem description consists of four steps:

1. Illustration of symptoms or problem behavior.
2. Addition of causes.
3. Evaluation of the relationship between causes and symptoms.
4. Identification of additional contextual factors that cannot be modified.

First, problematic behavior (symptoms) is extracted from patient exploration. No more than three symptom areas should be identified. In our example, the stress response in a work situation serves as the central symptom requiring treatment. Stress is understood as a cluster of symptoms consisting of cognitive ('I will never make it!'), emotional ('I am scared'), and physiological responses ('I am sweating') as well as behaviors ('I am just sitting here'). Placed in a square box, 'stress' is added to the right side of the diagram (Rules 1 and 2, also see Figure 6.6).

Rule 1. The diagram should be read from left to right. Causes are listed on the left side, symptoms on the right.

Rule 2. The problem behaviors (symptoms) are symbolized by a square (☐).

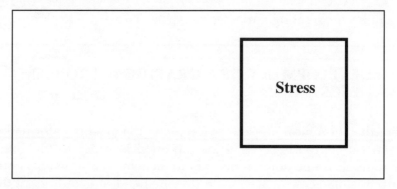

Figure 6.6   Patient symptoms

Second, presumed *causes* of this behavior are added. It is of particular importance that those aspects of problematic behavior are identified which can actually be influenced by therapeutic intervention. In our example, four factors seem to contribute to the problem: a high number of work tasks, lack of rest periods, an inefficient work style, and irrational beliefs. These four factors will be inserted into the diagram in accordance with Rule 3.

Rule 3. Causal and maintaining factors are symbolized by the oval (◯).

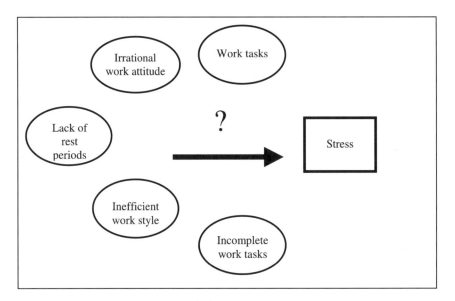

Figure 6.7 Adding in causal factors

Third, the relationships among the different causes and symptoms are inserted. The therapist highlights the relationships most crucial to the therapy by using thick arrows. Thus, Figure 6.8 will be modified according to Rule 4.

Rule 4. Direction and line width of arrows indicate causative significance of each factor in producing the symptoms.
Rule 5. The diagram should also reflect the sequence of factors in causing the symptoms.

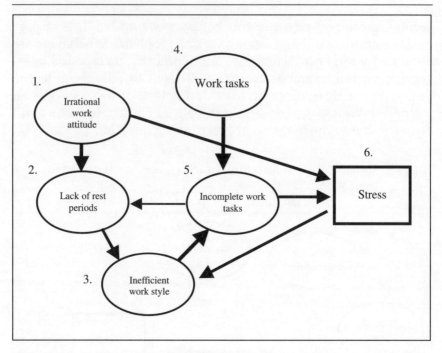

Figure 6.8 Adding in the relationships among factors represented by arrows

Each arrow in Figure 6.8 represents a clinically significant relationship. Different components are numbered. For example, '1→2' indicates that irrational beliefs lead to a lack of rest periods. The irrational work attitude finds its expression in the patient's belief that he must not take any breaks (1→2). Particularly, in situations with high work demands the patient does not allow himself to take breaks (5→2), and the lack of recreational breaks makes efficient work less likely (2→3). Consequently, fewer tasks will be completed (3→5). To sum up, a loop is identified connecting incomplete work, lack of rests and bad working style (5→2→3→5). This inefficient work style is exacerbated by the fact that the patient now feels distressed, which in turn renders him incapable of any work (6–3). Still he finds himself in a situation where he must also cope with the additional demands of his supervisor and must complete even more tasks (4→5). The therapist considers the irrational beliefs about work as the most important factor in causing stress (1→6, 5→6).

Contrary to Haynes's model, in which line width of arrows reflects statistical relationships, in controlled practice use of graphical problem description line width of arrows indicates the degree of clinical significance.

As a final step, we can add in those contextual factors that are not modifiable (e.g. chronic health problems, childhood experiences). Adjustments to significant life events may also trigger the symptoms. The therapist should be aware of these factors and may include them in the graphical problem description (see Rule 6).

Rule 6. Conditions that cannot be modified, such as experiences in the past, are labeled with a diamond ($\Diamond$).

Having set up the graphical problem description, we need to ask how well the description represent a problem, but this depends on a number of factors:

- whether the observations reported by the patients are correct;
- whether the problem is relatively stable and can be monitored during therapy;
- whether all essential relationships have been covered by the model;
- whether new situations do not produce incongruent facts.

When these conditions are met, a graphical problem description can be considered a valid representation of a client's problem, and can then serve as a basis for ensuing steps in controlled practice.

Chapter 7

A GRAPHICAL TREATMENT EXPLANATION

7.1 ABOUT THIS CHAPTER

To the outsider psychotherapy may appear vague and obscure. That is why it is important for therapists to be able to explain what they do and why they are doing it. The process of justifying therapeutic interventions occupies a central position in quality assurance effort since improvement is based on it. A vast amount of factors can be identified that affect the justification of therapeutic action (see Figure 7.1).

Therapy planning is always related to the disorder for which a patient seeks help; it depends on both the disorder's etiology and the current problem situation. Patients' attributes, including their resources and skills, have to be recognized when planning the therapy. How diagnostic information is treated and interpreted depends largely on the therapist's theoretical approach and personal style to conduct therapy. Also, the therapist's clinical experience and specialization have an impact on the selection of interventions that can be offered to the patients. Contextual factors such as opportunities for professional information exchange and mutual peer supervision considerably determine how the therapist proceeds. Finally, modifications may become necessary over the

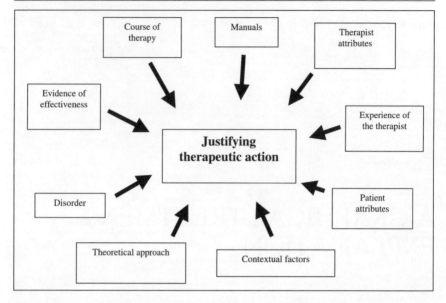

Figure 7.1 Factors influencing the justification of therapeutic action

course of therapy, and are unforeseeable at the outset. All of these factors are part of the effectiveness concept that therapists develop. Effectiveness concepts include all of the therapists' explanations and justifications that refer to type, duration, and expected side-effects of their interventions. As a consequence, therapists need to state twice, at the beginning and after completion of therapy

(1) what they are going to do
(2) why they intend to do it
(3) whether they have done it
(4) how they have done it, and
(5) the results they have accomplished.

Items (3) and (4) point to difficulties in the documentation of clinical practice; i.e. that the therapist does not adhere to the proposed treatment plan (problems of 'adherence' or 'integrity: Yeaton & Sechrest, 1981), or that the therapist is not sufficiently competent to put the plan into action (problem of 'competence': Waltz et al., 1993). Assuming a reasonable degree of treatment integrity, therapists may wish to use graphical methods in their efforts to justify their therapeutic approach.

7.2   ON THERAPY JUSTIFICATION

Who requests or needs a justification of the therapy plan?

In any case, therapists need to be able to explain to their patients how they expect the therapy to work; patients demand a well-founded therapy that provides for realistic outcome expectations. The payer or purchaser of the therapy is primarily interested in calculating the cost–benefit relations of psychotherapy.

Description of the therapy plan

Prior to justifying their treatment approach therapists need to describe and document what they intend to do. In clinical practice descriptions of therapy plans may vary significantly, for example, in terms of detail and standardization (e.g. use of manuals). Standardized approaches must be explained and justified in detail, both in terms of the overall approach and the distinctive parts of the therapy (e.g. intervention techniques, modules). Some cases only require use of a single and theoretically founded intervention while other situations require a combination of multiple techniques (as, for instance, in our example). The description of the procedure may then be limited to a statement on how the intervention techniques have been used.

In situations where therapists are not able to, or do not wish to, use evidence-based methods they need to describe thoroughly the methods they have developed themselves or adopted from colleagues. The less standardized their therapeutic approach, the more effort therapists must show to justify and explain their treatment plans.

How do therapists prove effectiveness?

In future it may not be sufficient to point out that planned psychotherapies are generally efficient. Today therapists may have to back up statement of effectiveness with scientific studies that provide evidence for specific therapy plans. The demonstration of efficiency, i.e. the superiority of one treatment approach over another, is also desirable.

In most instances empirical studies test the effectiveness of a particular intervention technique, as for example, progressive muscle relaxation or social skill training. These techniques are usually modified slightly for application in clinical practice or are used in combination on a case by case basis. The usefulness of empirical evidence for the justification of treatment plans depends largely on the degree of accuracy with which the therapists have described the interventions and the extent to which they adhere to them. It is important to keep the following critical points in mind:

1. Generalizability of empirical results to a specific therapy (validity)
2. Exact description and execution of the therapy plan
3. Therapist's competency to carry out the therapy plan
4. The correct referral of patients to specific treatment approaches (differential indication).

In applying intervention packages (manuals) to individual cases it becomes evident that these are not effective per se, since they widely ignore the patient's idiosyncrasies. This exposes a general weakness of many empirically supported approaches. Paul (1967) referred to the specific nature of empirical evidence in the following words (see Box 7.1):

Box 7.1   Differential Indication according to Paul (1967: 111; italics in original)

'*What* treatment, by *whom*, is most effective for *this* individual with *that* specific problem, and under *which* set of circumstances?'

According to Paul, a number of conditions influence the expectations of how effective or efficient a treatment will be. It is this complexity of conditions relevant for success that magnify the practical problems around the therapy's execution (Stiles, Shapiro & Elliott, 1986). For example, with 400 types of therapeutical intervention technique and about 150 different kinds of disorder, one will be faced with a vast number of combinations (Garfield & Bergin, 1994). In some specifications, like therapists' or patients' characteristics, a solution is becoming more and more difficult (Stiles, Shapiro & Elliott, 1986).

How can therapists justify their therapy plans?

Reference to empirical studies is a possible method of justifying the therapy plan, but it is more appropriate to explain the working theory behind the therapy plan. This calls for theoretical explanations, and a therapist has two options:

(a) He or she explains why the proposed therapy plan is appropriate and the changes that are to be expected.
(b) He or she refers to an external explanation, e.g. manuals.

Referring to experts, authorities, the tradition of the house, or a personal feeling is not satisfactory, and in any case an explanation has to be attainable. We now want to clarify the term 'working theory' and the meaning of a 'A graphical treatment explanation' (cf. Box 7.2).

Box 7.2   A graphical treatment explanation

A graphical treatment explanation describes in a graphical manner the essential thoughts of the therapist on how the problems of the patient could be overcome with the intervention techniques. Because the therapist takes several circumstances of the patient's situation into account, he or she discloses the idea and conceptions of why the proposed therapy plan should work (= working theory).

Before any explanation can be given, however, the therapy plan has first to be described.

7.3   THERAPY DOCUMENTATION

The description of a therapeutic effort consists of two parts: (1) a written plan for the therapy and (2) a graphic representation of the working theory (Box 7.3).

Box 7.3   Therapy description

A **therapy plan** is a written description of the intervention. It contains:

- diagnosis, including a description of the problem (see also 'graphical problem description')
- functional analysis
- goal analysis
- *intervention techniques*
- *time frame* of their application in therapy
- *structure* of the therapy

The working theory is also known as the 'graphical treatment description'. It contains:

- *problem areas* of the patient
- *causes and conditions* of the disorder
- *intervention techniques* used
- illustration of the *connection between intervention techniques and the problems* of the patient (working theory).

The parts of the therapy description build upon each other and serve different functions. A written therapy plan provides details on the patient, the problem or behavioral analysis, and the goals of the patient. It is sometimes also used in applications for funding. The therapy structure table serves as a guideline during therapy and as a description of treatment for single-case observation.

The table is also useful for quick comparisons of therapies, as it does not contain patient-specific information. The graphical treatment description explains the therapist's ideas on how the chosen intervention techniques can contribute to resolution of the patient's problems. This will be particularly useful for the interpretation of graphic curves at a later stage.

The primary elements of the therapy plan are illustrated through examples in Box 7.4 (elements not covered here include patient biography, disorder etiology, familial context, professional situation, etc.).

The therapy structure table breaks the therapy plan into a timed sequence of steps. Building the therapy structure table helps the therapist to estimate the time frame and frequency of sessions necessary, which is useful both for estimating costs and for motivating the patient. The table gives the patient an idea of what is possible, thus enabling him to form realistic expectations. It also assists the therapist in explaining the therapeutic techniques to be used; transparency of a table means that the patient can experience the therapy as an open process. The table form of description is better than a list at showing how various intervention steps overlap (see Table 7.1).

The therapy structure table is useful to formulate learning phases and to plan data collection (e.g. in determining the number and distribution of collection times); furthermore, it is possible to identify intermediate goals and to interpret therapy progress.

Table 7.1   Therapy structure table: sample case

Timeline	First consultation, therapy planning	First phase of therapy	Second phase of therapy	Third phase of therapy	End of therapy, follow-up
Contents of therapy	Case history Behavior analysis	Progressive muscle relaxation			Return visit/ discussion
		Acquisition of workplace-related social skills			
	Listing of priorities		Acquisition of social skills	Acquisition of working techniques	
Individual case study	Treatment questionnaire	Data collection/monitoring/control of intermediate goals			Evaluation

---

Box 7.4   Written therapy plan—sample case

- *Description of the disorder*: Due to excessive demands at work and related mental and physical exhaustion (evidenced by lack of concentration, sleep disorders), the patient decided to seek treatment. The patient complains of increasing demands at work, which he experiences mainly as the feeling of being unable to handle the work load.
- *Analysis of the disorder*: The patient's difficulties are the result of mutually reinforcing factors. The lack of rest periods results in work not being dealt with efficiently, which in turn leads to overtime and increased effort. This, in turn, deprives the patient of necessary resting periods. The unfavorable work conditions are the primary causes of the disorders, as they affect work techniques and mental fitness. As such, they must be changed.
- *Goal analysis*: Delegation of work, improved capability for relaxation, improved working techniques.
- *Therapy plan*: The patient needs to acquire the skill to recognize work that does not fall under his purview (= work-related competence) and to delegate it to coworkers (= social competence). Work techniques, such as making priority lists, should be practiced to increase efficiency. The patient must learn to take necessary rest breaks and to practice relaxation techniques consciously (= self-management). All in all he must reorganize his daily routine to include fixed rest periods and concrete relaxation exercises as a matter of course.

t_1: First consultation, introductory phase, case history
t_2: Analysis of problem or behavior
t_3: Generation of therapy plan
t_4: Relaxation exercises
t_5: Acquisition of social skills
t_6: Acquisition of work techniques
t_7: Concluding discussion
t_8: Follow-up

7.4   CAUSALITY CONCEPTS IN THERAPY PLANNING

The causality concepts covered in Chapter 6 were applied not only to formulate precise descriptions of disorders but also to specify the working theory. The intervention–effect concept is the equivalent of the stimulus–response concept discussed in Chapter 6. In the following we show how ideas of the therapist can be structured with the help of causality concepts. If the therapist wants to influence only one symptom with a single intervention technique, a specific intervention–effect concept is used.

In our example, the training of problem-solving techniques should impact only the patient's ability to cope with his work load. It would be a positive side effect if a change in other areas of behavior occurred on the basis of this self-management strategy. In this case, we speak of *broad-effect concept*. This term describes an intervention effecting more than one symptom at a time.

Primarily, this kind of broad effect is expected of intervention techniques such as relaxation training, i.e. progressive muscle relaxation. The same holds true for problem-solving techniques. The therapist could assume that, due to the acquired problem-solving techniques, not only is the job performance influenced but also the attitude toward work. A realistic assessment of the task is part of a successful problem solution. Moreover, the therapist might expect a reduction in the impact of stress as an indirect effect of the problem-solving techniques. In this case, the therapist has to assume a *transfer-effect concept* (intervention > change > effect). If the therapist uses several intervention techniques simultaneously—for example, a combination of pharmacological and behavioral treatment—then *multifactorial-effect concepts* apply. This short statement on the use of causality concepts for the founded decision of an intervention illustrates the advantage of causality concepts for a single-case description.

The explanation of an intervention effect can be more precise with an additional indication of theory, i.e. referring to the behavioral theory approach or analytic theory approach. In our example, the problem-solving   techniques   are   based   on   a   theory   by

Meichenbaum. Progressive muscle relaxation can be attributed to Jacobson, and, when discussing changes of irrational beliefs, Ellis has to be quoted.

It is obvious that you cannot combine any theoretical bases for the explanation. Of course the grounds of a therapy plan are simplified if only a single theoretical approach, with no additional theoretical school, is referred to. The therapeutical approach reaches purity if intervention techniques based on a single theoretical approach are used ('Purity'; Luborsky, 1984).

7.5   STEPS TOWARDS A GRAPHICAL TREATMENT EXPLANATION

We now turn to the steps involved in generating a graphical treatment explanation which

- requires little effort
- conveys the therapist's intent to the patient
- permits a quick overview into the therapeutic approach for third parties
- deals with the complexity of the matter
- is easy to document.

Procedure

Let us return to our example from Chapter 6, which was developed in three steps. First, the next step is added in the graphical problem description, i.e. the goals of intervention (the gray elements in Figure 7.2). The 'graphical problem description' is supplemented with an additional graphical element (triangle △) symbolizing one of each of these intervention techniques:

- Assertiveness training
- Counselling on attitude toward work
- Progressive muscle relaxation
- Problem-solving techniques

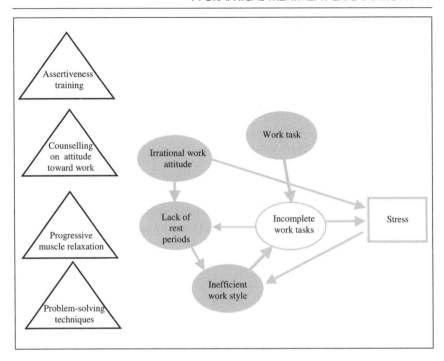

Figure 7.2 Addition of intervention techniques

Rule 7. The aims of therapeutic action are underlined gray in the graphical problem description.

Rule 8. Intervention techniques are symbolized by triangles (△).

The therapist has now to indicate the effects of intervention techniques on the different problem areas, and the following questions must be answered:

1. Which problem areas are influenced directly or indirectly by the intervention techniques?
2. How do the intervention techniques complement each other in their effect (cognitive, emotional, or behavioral effect)?
3. Do the intervention techniques differ in their grade of effect on the problem area, i.e. can the side effects and main interventions be differentiated?
4. Which side effects of the intervention techniques are to be expected?

To answer the first question the intervention techniques (triangles) get connected to the problem cause (bold ovals). In our example, the intervention technique 'progressive muscle relaxation' has one specific goal: the creation of 'rest periods'. Accordingly, counseling on attitudes towards work are expected to modify irrational beliefs. The intervention techniques 'social skills training' and 'work techniques' also directly and specifically target one cause of the disorder, and we can therefore speak of specific-effect models.

The intervention techniques aim at different levels: relaxation training affects physical symptoms, while the cognitive reorganization changes the attitude to work. By problem-solving and the assertiveness training a new competence on the behavior level should be obtained. In our example, there are no differentiated expectations concerning the strength of the intervention techniques, i.e. we do not distinguish between side effects and main effects. Nevertheless the patient has doubts about losing time in applying the new skills at work; this is time that he needs to fulfill his work tasks. The therapist accepts these doubts of the patient and displays them as part of an irrational belief of work. The therapist reaches an agreement with the patient that the new skills should enable him to cope better with his work load. This example shows how important it is to take the doubts about the side-effects of the intervention techniques seriously; because a therapy plan can only be implemented correctly if the patient is willing to comply.

The therapist now adds arrows of effects as in Figure 7.3 according to Rules 9 through 12.

Rule 9. The effect of the intervention techniques are represented by arrows.

Rule 10. The thickness of the arrows symbolizes the expected effect; the arrows used for side effects should be thinner than those used for main effects.

Rule 11. Side-effects are symbolized by thin lines.

Rule 12. Transfer effects can be represented as dotted lines, without overloading the graphic.

As more details are added to the 'graphical treatment explanation' over the process of therapy, the therapist can present and explain this representation of the mechanism of action to the patient again.

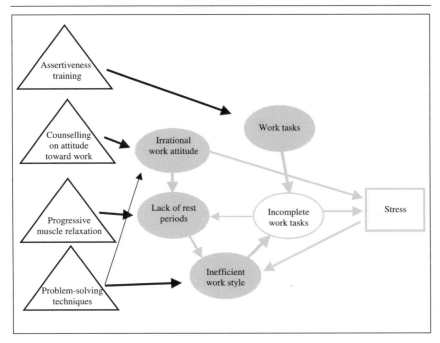

Figure 7.3 Connection of intervention techniques and problem causes

7.6 LIMITATIONS OF FIGURES

All details only illustrate a small part of human experience and behavior. On the one hand, limits arise on the quantity of information, observations, and assessments which have been collected about the patient's problems and goals. On the other hand, any model is only valid if the life situation of the patient does not change during therapy. At this point the temporary nature of the illustration must be stressed again.

It is a fundamental requirement of our graphical treatment explanation that the therapist is willing and able to make implicit thoughts explicit. The individual features of the single case have to be taken into account by the therapist while planning the therapy. This chapter aimed at conveying techniques with which the therapist can, step by step, document, justify, and optimize his action and behavior. From this fund of documented practical experiences many ideas may arise on how therapeutical changes can be obtained and explained more easily.

Chapter 8

THERAPY PROCESS QUESTIONNAIRE

8.1 ABOUT THIS CHAPTER

This chapter deals with the development of a therapy process questionnaire. As indicated in Chapter 2, the core consideration of an individual case analysis pertains to data collection. The requirements shown in Box 8.1 should be met.

Box 8.1   Requirements of therapy process questionnaires in controlled practice

The therapy process questionnaire should:

- relate to all important *therapy effects*;
- check the *intervention techniques* for their effectiveness;
- be *informative* for the patient as well as the therapist;
- be *suitable for everyday application*;
- outline the characteristics of the therapy process *precisely* and *economically*;
- be easy to *evaluate*;
- be *inexpensive*.

Not all of the demands in Box 8.1 can reasonably be expected to be met simultaneously, particularly if hardly more than half an hour is available in practice for construction. Nevertheless, the ability to develop or adapt a process questionnaire is a learnable skill. Here we offer step-by-step instructions, and although they do not guarantee that a questionnaire will live up to all requirements in every case, the procedure suggested should minimize the risk of failure.

This questionnaire is of fundamental importance for individual case studies. Mistakes made while generating the process questionnaire are unlikely to be corrected later. The therapist should therefore follow these steps very carefully (see Box 8.2).

Box 8.2   Steps for the development of a process questionnaire

1. Determine the content.
2. Set up a suitable standardized test.
3. Select items from the standardized test.
4. Add your own questions.
5. Determine the number of response formats per question.
6. Design the questionnaire.
7. Test the questionnaire and check comprehensibility.
8. Set up an analysis system (assigning numerical values to response formats).

8.2   CONTENTS OF THE QUESTIONNAIRE

First, the therapist must determine the content of the process questionnaire. Two questions can help to solve this problem:

1. Which symptoms should be included? For example, which characteristics/symptoms of stress are decreasing?
2. Which behavioral changes should be recorded? For example, does the patient make use of newly acquired problem-solving techniques in daily life?

In his or her analysis the therapist can ensure that not only the symptoms but also their underlying causes have been addressed.

Determining the effectiveness of therapy requires that outcomes are in fact attributable to it. Patients are primarily concerned with a cessation of their symptoms. From the therapist's point of view it is even more important to understand how the therapy works. Only by establishing that functional assumptions hold true can therapists be sure to replicate interventions successfully in future.

In drawing up the content of the process questionnaire therapists may scrutinize the graphical treatment explanation. Here, many of the core problem attributes and symptoms, as well as intervention techniques, are already laid out. The following selection of therapy characteristics taken from our example in Chapter 5 is used to illustrate this:

- Does the patient use his new skills (problem-solving techniques, progressive muscle relaxation)?
- Does the patient's stress decrease during the course of the therapy?
- Does work satisfaction increase due to a changed attitude toward work?
- Does the patient succeed in setting limits on his work load?

Figure 8.1 relates these questions to topics in the graphical treatment explanation; the elements shown in gray can be included in the process questionnaire. The upper section of Figure 8.1 displays the effects of intervention techniques, while the lower section lists the behavioral changes achieved.

The figure clarifies those therapy characteristics that are considered important by both patient and therapist. It also serves to explain the relevance of questions to the patient. In enabling patients to monitor critical changes throughout the therapy, high content validity can be achieved.

Besides behavioral changes and symptoms additional variables may be included in the questionnaire depending on the therapist's or the patient's interest. Items, for example, can relate to the quality of cooperation between patient and therapist—a crucial component for therapeutic success. The questionnaire provides patients with the opportunity to give *feedback on the the therapist's work* or to

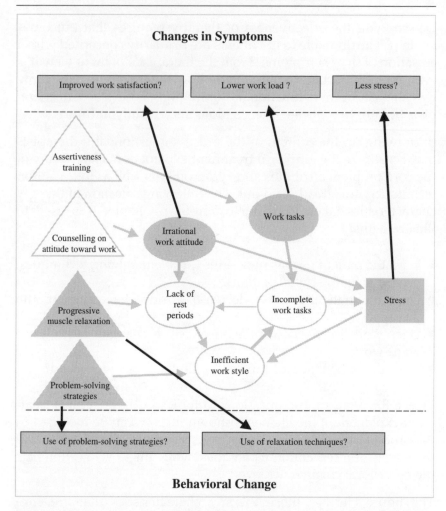

Figure 8.1 Questions derived from the graphical treatment explanation. (The black arrows indicate measurement-related connections between the constructs and their operationalizations)

rate the quality of the therapist–patient interaction. Examples of instruments that allow a patient-centered assessment of individual treatment sessions are the Session Evaluation Questionnaire (SEQ; Stiles et al., 1994) and the Session Impact Scale (SIS; Elliot & Wexler, 1994). The SEQ includes different oppositional adjectives that patients rate on 7-point Likert scales (for example, 'This session was . . .', 'Right now I feel . . .'). In addition, patients are asked to rate their current *motivation* and compliance. If the therapy seems likely to be terminated prematurely (for example, in the case of drug addiction or substance abuse) this type of systematic feedback enables therapists to uncover patients' problems to cooperate at an early stage in the therapy.

A fourth area is concerned with *external influences* that may affect the therapy. Patients may expect significant changes in their social environment; for example, job loss and other events that may impact their symptoms without actually being part of the therapy. The assessment of these liminal circumstances and context variables is important for understanding therapy efficacy. Clearly, the modification of symptoms is only attributable to these effects when other influences such as intervening life events can be ruled out.

8.3 WORDING OF QUESTIONS

The therapist transforms the most salient content features into questions (items). This collection of items should be answered regularly during therapy. Therapists have two options: they can either use well-known instruments or formulate their own questions. Both strategies will be presented here along with their advantages and disadvantages.

Selection of tests

Descriptions of tests can be found in the twelfth *Mental Measurement Yearbook* (Conoley & Impara, 1995), *Test Critiques* (Keyser & Sweetland, 1985), *Tests: A Comprehensive Reference for Assessment in Psychology, Education and Business* (Sweetland & Keyser, 1991) and *Measures for Clinical Practice: A Sourcebook* (Corcoran & Fischer, 1994). Beutler, Wakefield and Williams (1994) and Newman and Ciarlo (1994) cite some selected criteria for tests that are shown in Box 8.3.

According to Haynes (1993) it is difficult for therapists to find a suitable questionnaire for individualized therapies; they are scarce. As he states, 'Many psychological assessment instruments are

---

Box 8.3   Criteria for selecting tests (from Newman & Ciarlo, 1994)

1. Relevance to target group
2. Simple teachable methods
3. Use of measures with objective referents
4. Use of multiple respondents
5. More process-identifying outcome measures
6. Psychometric strength
7. Low measure costs relative to its benefits
8. Understanding by nonprofessional audiences
9. Useful in clinical services
10. Compatible with clinical theories and practice

---

poorly constructed, unreliable, unvalidated, invalid, and inappropriately applied. The integration of assessment data into treatment decisions remains one of the least researched aspects of applied psychology' (p. 251). When a therapist does find a suitable instrument, rules should guide the selection of items to be included in the process questionnaire.

Item selection

Therapists begin by asking these two questions:

1. Does the selected question correspond to the *content* of the formulated problem? Here the therapist needs to discuss with the patient those questions that can be chosen from the questionnaire's item pool.
2. Does the selected question display sound psychometric properties? Test manuals provide answers to the question of how well the item correlates with the overall scale. Such an item should be well above average compared to other items. A high correlation indicates, on one hand, that the item measures sufficiently accurately, i.e. is reliable, and, on the other, how well it represents the entire test.

In general, this procedure is rather time consuming to the therapist because it entails selecting and later evaluating several different tests. Because of these difficulties, we encourage therapists to work with their patients to formulate appropriate content-specific questions.

Development of one's own questions

Therapists have several options to formulate questions, only some of which will be discussed here (see Box 8.4).

Box 8.4   Different forms of questions

(a) *Verbal or nonverbal*
- Written form: I feel well today!
- Nonverbal form: ☹   ☺   ☺

(b) *Open vs closed format*
- Open format: I feel . . . . today.
- Closed format: On a scale of 1–10, today I feel
                           happy: _____

(c) *Global vs specific*
- Global: I feel well.
- Specific: Today I had a successful
                           experience at work.

(d) *Direct vs indirect*
- Direct: I feel better today than
                           yesterday . . . (0 = no change)
- Indirect: On a scale of 1 (bad) – 10
                           (well), today I felt: _____

Nonverbal items may be an alternative for patients with limited verbal abilities, but their content is difficult to represent graphically. Open format questions provide patients with the opportunity to give feedback on therapy sessions, and do allow for comments. However, as this type of question is not very suitable for systematically recording changes, preference should be usually given to closed format questions. Global forms of questions cover a wide-ranging content and are therefore more economical than specific questions. They are also somewhat more general, as they leave it to patients to decide which specific aspect to favor for evaluation. For example, therapists and patients can rate the extent of depression or other specific problems on a 9-point Likert scale, ranging from 'much worse' (–4) to 'much better' (+4) (see Jones et al., 1993). Aided by Clinical Global Impressions (CGI; Guy, 1976), therapists can determine impairment on a scale ranging from 0 to 7 for the last week.

A measurement of change can also be either *direct* or *indirect* (Bereiter, 1963). Direct questions require patients to assess whether changes have occurred. Indirect questions call for patients to evaluate their current state of health at two points in time. From the difference between two measurements the therapist determines actual change (see Figure 8.2).

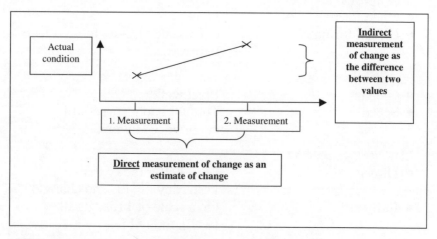

Figure 8.2   Direct and indirect measurement of change

The Goal Attainment Scale (GAS), which may be used in addition to process questionnaires, produces estimates of change pertaining to progress toward the goals set at the beginning of therapy. We will return to this issue at the end of this chapter.

The presented options of item formulation reflect the variety of opportunities that therapists have in designing a process questionnaire. We now give some hints on how to avoid common mistakes in the formulation of questions. Positive examples are marked +, negative are identified by – (see Box 8.5).

Box 8.5   Tips for the formulation of questions

1. *Use short items rather than long ones because they lessen the risk of ambiguity*
   - 'In general I find that I am satisfied with my work'
   + 'I am satisfied with my work'

2. *Use simple words rather than technical terms because they reduce the risk of misunderstandings*
   - 'My external locus of control has improved'
   + 'I am able to change things'

3. *Focus on observable behaviors rather than global estimates because they are more accurate*
   - 'I feel that I have rewarded myself today'
   + 'I went to the movies/for ice cream/for a walk today as a reward'

4. *Use exact response formats rather than open format items because they are more suitable to treatment evaluation*
   Question: Have you done the exercises today?
   - 'More than usual' . . . 'approximately the same' . . . 'less than usual'
   + 'I practiced _____ minutes today'

5. *Avoid appraisals in questions*
   - 'Naturally, I didn't do my exercises today either'
   + 'I did _____ exercises today'

6. *Use various response levels*
   - 'I am less stressed'
   + 'I have fewer hot flashes'; 'I have everything under control'; 'I am relaxed'

Whenever possible external evaluations should supplement sub-jective statements by the patient. Therapists can also evaluate changes from their point of view, or a friend of the patient can be asked to validate the patient's observations.

Development of response formats

For each question a response format needs to be developed. Box 8.6 presents tips for developing response formats with positive (+) and negative (−) examples.

Box 8.6   Tips for the formulation of replies

1. *Response formats should be unambiguous*
   - once per day   several times per week
   + _____ exercises per week (number)

2. *Response formats should reflect extreme changes*
   - Got better   unchanged   got worse
   + Got much better   got better   unchanged   got worse   got much worse

3. *Response formats should be sufficiently differentiated*
   - yes   no
   + definitely true   true   neither–nor   not true   definitely not true

4. *Response formats should be easy to analyze*
   - less than one minute   less than half an hour   several hours
   + _____ minutes (number)

If patients experience great changes in their symptoms, they must be able to express that in the questionnaire. Therefore, even 'un-likely' answers should not be left out.

'Anchoring' of the scales

It is recommended that therapists talk with their patients about questionnaire formats, in particular if they rely heavily on the patient for symptom monitoring. This may help patients to become more familiar and comfortable with the instrument. It is also necessary that therapist and patient together establish numerical values for each possible response in each question. This process can be called 'anchoring' of scales. Thurstone and Cave advanced this technique as early as 1929 and applied it to the measurement of attitudes within social psychology. The principle of assigning numerical values to phenomena under investigation can also be applied to observable behavior. The same holds true for the assessment of physiological responses. We illustrate this process in Figure 8.3.

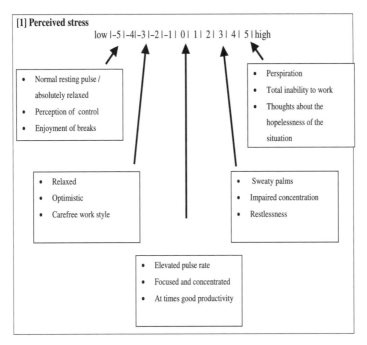

Figure 8.3   Assessment of perceived stress: physiological, cognitive and behavioral indicators

Throughout the therapy the patient can always refer to the decisions made earlier on how to assign numerical codes to observations. Modifications of the scale may become necessary, for instance, if work-related stress increases to a degree that the patient in our example ceases to work at all.

8.4 DESIGNING THE QUESTIONNAIRE

Having determined a pool of questions and answers, the therapist now designs the questionnaire, making sure that its length does not exceed one sheet. In keeping the instrument brief, therapists avoid overburdening their patients and circumvent the risk of demotivation. As a rule of thumb, only such information should be collected that can actually be used. As a consequence, therapists should not ask more than ten questions. A structure layout helps to avoid mistakes during completion and analysis of the questionnaire. The following questionnaire has been designed for our example case (see Figure 8.4). Coding information has been added to enable individual cases to be tracked throughout their therapy.

Patient Code:
Special events

---

[1] **Experience of stress**
  low | –5 | –4 | –3 | –2| –1 | 0 | 1 |2 | 3 | 4 | 5| high

[2] **Work satisfaction**
  low | –5 | –4 | –3 | –2| –1 | 0 | 1 |2 | 3 | 4 | 5| high

[3] **Work load**
  low | –5 | –4 | –3 | –2| –1 | 0 | 1 |2 | 3 | 4 | 5| high

[4] **Use of relaxation therapy during work. How often per week?**
  0 | 1 |2 | 3 | 4 | 5| 6 | 7 | 8 | 9 | 10 _____times

[5] **Use of problem solving techniques during work. How often per day?**
  0 | 1 |2 | 3 | 4 | 5| 6 | 7 | 8 | 9 | 10 _____times

Figure 8.4 Example for a process questionnaire

Trial-run of the instrument

It is advisable to have the patient fill out the questionnaire once as a test to discuss any difficulties that might occur in completing it.

Analysis

If the questionnaire has been designed in accordance with the aforementioned recommendations, no particular problems should arise during the analysis. However, handling questionnaires that contain open response format items may be somewhat more difficult to analyze. Transfer of the responses into a computerized database usually requires some type of coding, i.e. the transformation of qualitative responses into numerical values. Quantifying responses will in turn allow the therapist to produce graphs that displays developments over time. Multiple response formats are less ambiguous than open scale questions. Another set of practical problems occurs if patients forget to fill out questionnaires. These 'missing data' may be smoothed over in the evaluation by either entering the status of the previous day or by computing average values from past observations.

8.5   GOAL ATTAINMENT SCALE: A SUPPLEMENTAL METHOD

The goals of the patient occupy a central place in single-case diagnostics. The Goal Attainment Scale (GAS) is a method of assessing relevant outcomes in a practical way. Strictly speaking, the GAS is a procedure that facilitates the development of practice-based outcome measures that adequately reflect the patient's perspective.

Based on the idiographic method, the GAS was first developed by Kiesler (1966) and later improved by Suchman (1967). Other goal-oriented measures of therapy outcomes had previously been available—e.g. the Menninger Foundation Psychotherapy Research Project (Wallerstein et al., 1956, 1958), the method of Malan (1963), the Managing for Results model (Drucker, 1964), and the Target Complaints model (Battle et al., 1966).

The Goal Attainment Scale explicitly allows for the assessment of therapy goals based on the patient's needs. It permits the development of an individually tailored measurement instrument. The advantage of such an approach, as opposed to a standardized process, lies with its concerted attempt to gauge patient satisfaction. Unfortunately, patient satisfaction is not really a measurement of therapy success and can vary greatly between individuals. Some patients are quite satisfied if someone is listening to them, whether or not they reach a therapy goal, and other patients will still be dissatisfied even when most of the goals have been attained.

GAS addresses the demand for individualization in therapy evaluation (Kiesler, 1966). It was developed in the United States between 1970 and 1975 with a considerable financial investment of almost $1.5 million (Seaberg & Gillespie, 1977). Kiresuk and Sherman (1968) first introduced the GAS and it found a ready market in the USA. It is now one of the most frequently used therapy evaluation procedures. Wide usage has led to a large volume of publications on studies that have used GAS in nearly all areas of clinical psychology as well as health care and intervention research (see Kiresuk, Smith & Cardillo, 1994).

In the GAS, the therapist and patient establish the desired outcomes for the therapy, grouped into problem areas, prior to actual therapy. Next, they determine indicators for attainment of these goals. In general, five indicators are identified for each problem area. Indicators within a problem area are sorted according to the difficulty of attainment, with the most realistic goal in the center. Easier goals are listed before more difficult ones, and in this way a quantifiable scale can be obtained (see Table 8.1). Currently, the most common procedure is to coordinate goals with the patient, but the alternatives of having goals set by a co-therapist, a team of coworkers, or the patient alone have also been explored. Study results suggest that therapy motivation as well as therapy success increase when the patient is actively involved in the goal-setting process (see Kiresuk, Smith & Cardillo, 1994).

Table 8.1 shows the operationalization of outcome indicators in a case of test anxiety. The outcome that can be most realistically expected is that the student will be very nervous before the exam and will experience increasing anxiety with the exam date approaching, is extremely nervous and anxious during the exam itself, but takes it nonetheless. The negative values represent worse alternatives; items with positive values represent a greater therapy success than could be expected.

Table 8.1 Clarification of a protocol sheet for GAS evaluation (example: test anxiety)

Value	Outcome indicators	Area: Test anxiety
−2	Definitely less than expected	Starts sweating at the thought of an exam—does not register for an exam
−1	Somewhat less than expected	Registers and prepares for the exam, but the closer the exam gets the greater the phobia—cancels immediately before the exam
0	Expected outcome	Increasing phobia with approaching exam date—takes exam with great fear
+1	Somewhat better than expected	Remains calm during preparation for exam, but still is nervous during the exam
+2	Definitely better than expected	Remains calm during preparation and exam

Classic GAS studies (Kiresuk & Sherman, 1968) weight different goals according to their relative importance, but this practice is now often disregarded. Instead, after a set period, it is evaluated whether predetermined goals have been accomplished. Additional follow-up assessments are useful to ensure long-term success. It is also necessary to determine whether the assessment should be conducted by the therapist (risking potential bias) or by an independent observer. Ideally, therapist and patient closely cooperate in evaluating the degree of goal attainment. In clinical trials outside observers should be asked to perform the evaluation.

As a first step in analysis, a total summary score is produced for all outcome indicators (scales). For example, if the student of Table 8.1 remains calm during preparations for her exam (score = 0) and only becomes nervous during the exam itself (score = 1), the total score would be 1. The total score can be t-transformed (see Kiresuk, Smith & Cardillo, 1994), permitting future inter-individual comparisons. These standardized values are expected to be distributed normally and to have a mean value of 50 (Kiresuk, Smith & Cardillo, 1994). Deviations of up to one standard deviation (10 points) mark average values; higher, or lower scores reflect outcomes above or below the expectations for the therapy.

The reliability of the GAS has been determined by interrater agreement studies. In some cases, these values are surprisingly high. The lowest estimate has been found to be 0.52, the highest 0.99. These coefficients depend on data homogeneity and rater qualifications. In studies at the Reno VA Medical Center, where raters are also trained, results varied between 0.78 and 0.99 (Kiresuk, Smith & Cardillo, 1994).

Generally speaking, validity studies for the GAS face the problem that, due to the strictly individual approach, almost no significant agreement with standardized measurement instruments can be expected. Therefore it is not surprising that results for comparative studies are not all uniform (Kiresuk, Smith & Cardillo, 1994). The measurement of variation is also problematic, because the GAS does not include a baseline measurement. Nonetheless, moderate correlations of 0.43 have been found between the GAS and independent clinical improvement ratings (Jacobs & Cytrynbaum, 1977; Kiresuk, Smith & Cardillo, 1994).

The use of the GAS for the evaluation of interventions seems acceptable in view of psychometric properties. The strength of the procedure lies with its specificity and the fact that negotiation about goals is part of therapy itself. The latter is designed to strengthen patients' therapy motivation and enhance therapists' self-reflections. Various authors have pointed out the therapeutic effect of the GAS: when a GAS procedure was used patients profited more from their therapy than control patients without the GAS (Houts & Scott, 1976; Galano, 1977; Laferriere & Callsyn, 1977).

As the development of a measurement instrument becomes part of the therapeutic process, confounding of the results cannot be entirely avoided if one does not want to sacrifice the positive effect of the joint goal negotiations. For comprehensive therapy evaluations it is therefore recommended to use standardized instruments in addition to the GAS.

Therapists should obtain training and have sufficient clinical experience before they use the GAS in their therapies. Its successful utilization largely depends on how well goals and treatment expectations are operationalized. Unrealistic estimates can bias results; for example, very optimistic therapists who have unrealistic expectations and choose goals that are far too ambitious are sure to achieve worse results than a therapist with a more pessimistic attitude. Further objections refer to the measurement level of the GAS in that scores from different items are added to summary scores interval scale level is assumed; in practice, however, this is rarely achieved (Seaberg & Gillespie, 1977). Further critique is directed toward the calculation of standard values: scale intercorrelations are estimated at 0.30. Naturally, these correlations cannot be empirically evaluated for individual cases. For applications in the clinical setting any of these objections is only of marginal importance.

The GAS is an economical tool that involves the patient in specifying the therapy goals. It is a method therapists and patients can use to structure their goals. Well-defined outcomes and structured operational goals facilitate the clinical work of the therapist. Furthermore, it equips therapists with strategies for self-evaluation that help them to ascertain whether their outcome expectations are realistic. During goal negotiations at the beginning of therapy patients learn to define goals for themselves. This can be considered a first valuable step toward a successful therapy.

Chapter 9

DATA COLLECTION

9.1 ABOUT THIS CHAPTER

This chapter will address the following features of data collection:

- General aspects of data collection
- Graphical formulation of hypotheses
- General aspects of data processing

Therapist and patient need to negotiate amount and frequency of assessment to go on in data collection. Phases of data collection need to be planned parallel to treatment delivery and to take into consideration the private situation of the patient. At the outset of therapy, the therapist should record his or her expectations as regards processual outcome-oriented aspects of therapy. Confirmation or refutation of these will produce evidence as to the appropriateness and effectiveness of the therapy. Since clinical practice does not allow for hypotheses to be formulated with the same rigor is common in other scientific fields (i.e. analysis is compromised in clinical practice alone from the fact that observer and analyst coincide in one person), some alternative methods by using a graphical description for hypotheses are in order. This chapter will conclude with some practical hints on effective data processing.

9.2 DATA COLLECTION

Yin (1984) conceptualizes research designs as action plans comprising five components: (1) a study question; (2) propositions, if any; (3) unit(s) of analysis; (4) the logical link between the data and the propositions; and (5) criteria for interpreting the findings.

There are two questions of primary importance in controlled practice. First, has therapy produced any of the anticipated changes and outcomes from the perspective of the patient (evaluation of outcome)? Second, has therapy worked as the therapist expected (evaluation of working theory)? In controlled practice the object of analysis is always observable change in the patient (unit = patient), or, put differently, changes that take place as a result of the close cooperation of patient and therapist (unit = patient + patient × therapist). Links between outcomes and therapy are illustrated by graphical treatment explanation (see Figure 8.1). While outcome evaluation is concerned primarily with the reduction of symptoms as a consequence of therapy (as specified in the patient's goals; see Figure 6.5), the therapist's main interest lies with how effectively particular intervention strategies produce certain changes in the patient's behavior. The therapist's expectations will be discussed later in this chapter. The evaluation plan also contains information on sampling times and frequencies (see 'Over- and under-sampling' in Chapter 10).

Figure 9.1 demonstrates the effect of ill-defined times of assessment, also known as the 'aliasing effect'. The centerline represents the actual changes accomplished by the patient. The curve above, based on a few ill-selected times of assessment, appears to indicate a continuous trend of improvement. On the other hand, one may be tempted to conclude that nothing has really happened if one simply looked at the curve below. In any case, the golden rule is to collect data more frequently rather than less, in order to avoid the risk of overlooking changes or misinterpreting chance effects.

Assessment frequency may vary in different phases of therapy. It is quite common for posttreatment follow-up assessment to occur far less frequently than measurement while in therapy. Nevertheless, 'stability checks' are a desirable feature of clinical practice if feasible (see Figure 9.2).

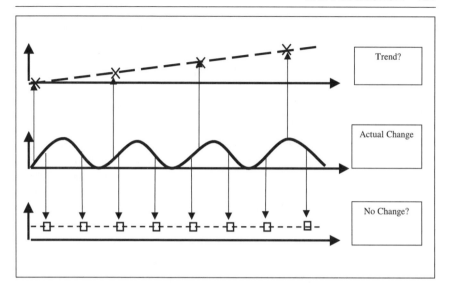

Figure 9.1 Mis-sampling and artifacts (aliasing effect)

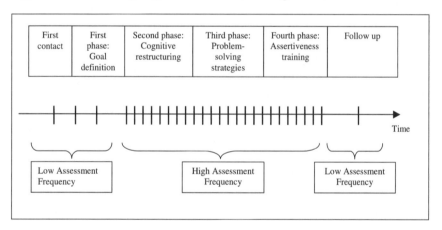

Figure 9.2 Number of assessments in different phases of therapy

It is a key feature of controlled-practice designs that therapy and interventions cannot be manipulated arbitrarily; all strategies are based on problem and outcome analysis. The therapist has first to decide whether unequivocal hypotheses can be devised for a particular therapy. If, for example, a therapy includes an array of many different intervention techniques that require little time each and are carried out in quick succession, it will be impossible to evaluate every detail of the therapy. There will be insufficient data for the testing of hypotheses.

Naturally, in clinical practice it is impossible to manipulate systematically all the factors in the therapy plan that may have an impact on patient behaviors and experiences. Therapy plans in clinical practice are usually quasi-experimental designs. Therapy-induced changes can be assessed at many different levels, which means that single-case studies resort to the use of multiple-baseline designs. Data collection designs for single-case analyses are covered in greater detail by, among others, Kazdin (1982, 1998), Herson and Barlow (1984), Franklin, Allison and Gorman (1997), and Kratochwill and Levin (1992).

9.3   EXPECTATIONS AND HYPOTHESES

In Chapter 5 we described how therapists formulate expectations concerning changes in the patient resulting from therapy. These expectations (or hypotheses) can later be compared with the empirical outcomes. It is very difficult to develop precise hypotheses, since knowledge about how and when a patient's situation will change is sketchy at the outset of therapy. We wish to make therapists aware of some of the particular features of therapeutic processes in order to ensure that clinical hypotheses can be tested adequately.

Choice of the measure of change must be based on the content of the patient's presenting problem: the patient's ultimate goal is to be free of symptoms *at the end* of therapy. It is of secondary importance which fluctuations in symptoms occur beforehand. The patient's expectations before and after therapy can be compared effectively by computing the respective means (see Figure 9.3 (a)). The therapist, on the other hand, is mainly interested in the changes that take place *during* therapy, in light of the expectation of continuous improvement of the patient's problem. This expectation is more adequately represented by average trends (Figure 9–3 (b)).

A change-in-level from pre- to post-test means is a crude but still useful indicator of goal attainment. Trend hypotheses reflect the

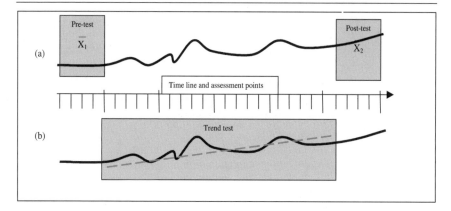

Figure 9.3   Hypotheses of change (hypotheses-relevant sections of the process are shaded)

direction of change rather than magnitude. Measuring goal attainment is the most crucial element in the evaluation of therapeutic success; trend hypotheses answer questions on the therapist's assumptions about his or her working theory of a therapy.

The formulation of hypotheses also depends widely on how the patient's critical condition is defined. If the patient complains about being emotionally unstable, the goal of therapy may not be a shift in the level of symptoms but rather a reduction of the emotional variability (see Figure 9.4 (a)). In another scenario, the patient may be plagued by attacks or flare-ups during periods of increased symptomatic activity. In this situation the therapist would attempt to shorten these active periods or to reduce the aversity of symptoms during periods of increased disease activity (Figure 9.4 (b)). In the first case, the therapist compares the fluctuations of symptoms during the first half of the therapy to those present in the second half. In the latter case systematic hypothesis-testing is almost impossible, and it may be advisable to resort to a visual inspection.

The four examples (Figures 9.3 and 9.4) were chosen to illustrate that hypotheses may be developed for different aspects of the therapy process. At the very least, therapists should try to roughly sketch their expectations of the course of therapy in order to compare them with intervention outcomes.

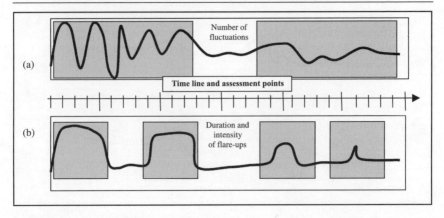

Figure 9.4   Hypotheses of change (shaded segments are relevant for the testing of hypotheses)

9.4   DATA PROCESSING

Data gathered by the process questionnaire require initial processing before hypotheses can be tested. We recommend that therapists follow the steps of action listed in Box 9.1.

Box 9.1   Steps of action in data analysis

1. Data entry
2. Data verification
3. Data processing
4. Hypothesis-guided analysis
5. Presentation of results
6. Documentation

First, answers from the questionnaire must be entered into a table. Questionnaire items are transformed into variables, and the patient's answers coded as numerical values. All codes need to be documented and explained in codebooks. This step also ensures that any future analysis of the data can be carried consistently. For example, with the help of the codebook, it will be possible to reconstruct that code '1' indicated 'was on type' for the variable 'compliance'. The uniform use of the coding system reduces the risk of misinterpretations and facilitates comparability between individual cases. Hence, we will make a few suggestions on how to code typical answer formats, and on the rules to be observed (see Box 9.2).

After all data have been coded they should be verified; that is, the data sets need to be checked for errors that may have occurred during data entry or that may have been transferred from the questionnaires into the database. This also includes an analysis of missing values, extreme values (see Chapter 10), and any other irregularities. If there are missing or 'invalid' values in the data set, these may be estimated on the basis of procedures described in detail in statistical textbooks. In general, data correction should be kept to a minimum, since any form of manipulation bears the risk of confounding results. However, evidence can be increased when several analysts, such as the patient and the therapist, reach an agreement on how to make sense of the data (i.e. validation through self-reports and observation).

As the first step in the analysis, statistical measures of central tendency (e.g. mean) and dispersion (e.g. variance) are computed. The use of diagrams (bar or pie charts and timelines) is recommended when statistical skills are rather limited. It is possible to test hypotheses using both graphical and statistical methods (see Chapter 10).

Aside from data that describe therapeutic course or process, information should be collected that captures contextual aspects of the therapy, such as patient, therapist, and setting characteristics. Chapter 11 covers the collection of these additional features.

Box 9.2   Codebook and answer formats

1. Dichotomous selection

Example: I worked today: □ Yes   □ No

Coding: Yes = '1'   analogous

Agreement
positive answer   }   = 1
male
I agree

Coding: No = '2'   analogous

Rejection
negative answer   }   = 2
female
I disagree

2. Rating formats

Example: My assertiveness has:
□ increased markedly □ increased □ not changed
□ decreased □ decreased markedly
Coding: increased markedly = 1   increased = 2   not changed = 3
decreased = 4   decreased markedly = 5
Rule: The first answer option is always coded '1', the following
answers are assigned increasing numbers.

3. Alternative answers (A *or* B)

Example: Today I: □ drove my car   □ rode my bike
□ used the train   □ walked
Coding: car = 1   bike = 2   train = 3   walked = 4

4. Multiple answers (A *and* B)

Example: Today I: □ went for a walk   □ went for a run
□ went to the movies   □ did other things
Coding: Every answer option is considered to be a separate
question and coded according to the dichotomous answer format:
Went for a walk: yes = 1   no = 2
Went for a run: yes = 1   no = 2, etc.

5. Quantitative answers

Examples: _____ Number of exercises per week
Coding: Immediate use of the number provided

Chapter 10

STATISTICAL ANALYSIS

Hans C. Waldmann

10.1 INTRODUCTION

Now that you have learned all about integrating strategies of controlled practice in your therapy planning and conduct, you are
faced with a chapter on *statistical analysis*. Why bother with statistics? You are a practitioner dedicated to deliver primary health
care to your clients. You are inclined to use the documentation
systems outlined in previous sections in order to further enhance
your services by monitoring your client's progress toward therapy
goals. But it's all there! You have collected data in a scientifically
conditioned setting; you have derived a set of hypotheses from
your client's problem analysis; you have defined several therapy
objectives that may translate into more formal effect sizes; you
virtually apply a carefully designed treatment; and you keep track
of the experiment. So why not take the last step and add scientific
merits to your client's benefits? There are a quite a few reasons
why you should engage in a final summary analysis, and this
chapter aims at convincing you that statistical analysis is readily
available and does not necessarily presuppose advanced command
of calculus. In our setting, data must be *understood* rather than
analyzed. Since this chapter is not intended to provide an introductory course in statistics in its own right, we must rely on your
familiarity with some basic concepts, such as random variables or

variance or the mechanics of chi-square tests. You will, however, be directed to suitable references.

We will begin by discussing preliminary decisions to be taken (setting up data structures, hypotheses formalization, etc.), give an overview of models suitable for the kind of data resulting from your documentation system and move on to present you with a selection of this set in more detail. Note that unlike most textbooks on the analysis of single-case data there will be no in-depth covering of 'real' time series analysis like ARIMA-models or intervention analysis. While there can be no doubt that these models are powerful tools, we still believe that they are only rarely appropriate for data assessed in real-life therapy situations and, in any case, may be far too demanding both in terms of computational resources and time required. You will find that we put much emphasis on feasibility and will always try to reconcile scientific analysis with your daily practice as a therapist.

10.2   DATA STRUCTURES AND HYPOTHESES

It is agreed that *analysis* may be conceived as the last step of a process of empirical research, a step that should perform the transition *from 'data' to 'information'* and that helps to reduce, or at least to account for, the uncertainty inherent to sampling (Waldmann, 1997). Therefore, and prior to considering the particulars of statistical testing, we must determine the kind of 'data' that are available from documentation procedures and the kind of 'information' we seek to obtain from them as a result of our analysis.

The first question usually boils down to the issue of *coding* your data, whereas the latter means *formalizing* your hypotheses into terms of a statistical model. The conjecture of 'improvement' may thus translate into a 'trend' hypothesis which would imply the application of a 'test of nonstationarity' (see below). Your questions are, then:

- Is there a shift in location over time (given data on an interval scale coded as numeric intensity values of finite range sampled at discrete points in time)?

- Do event frequencies or probabilities increase over time (given binary/polytoneous/count data coded as success indicator/ categorical dummy/event count per time interval)?

Don't bother! You'll find out quickly that procedures are not quite as complicated as statisticians' jargon. Note that these are omnibus hypotheses that call for further differentiation: is there a linear/ monotonic trend (shape)?; does variability increase with location shift (stability)?; how about serial correlation (dependence) etc.?— just to mention a few for the metric data case. We will return to these issues in later sections. The important point lies with the fact that your coding method implies the set of formalization options and, as a consequence, delimits the set of suitable statistical models. In this chapter, we will mostly confine analysis to the *omnibus level*.

If you have assessed a criterion variable on an interval scale ranging from, say, 1 to 6, or from -3 to $+3$ for displaying a bipolar profile, you obtain *metric data*. Such data commonly arise from *rating state intensity*, although scale properties are only rarely tested for. There is not a great deal of coding effort: you simply associate the value with (a) measurement occasion or time, (b) a second variable for the treatment phase (baseline, treatment A, or B, etc.), and (c) potentially other criterion variables in order to assess their mutual interrelation or to test for latency in effect instantiation. Note that coding design information in (b) may require more than one variable (e.g. multiple baseline designs) and that a design variable may, instead of being a dummy indicator for presence or absence of treatment, take any value on the real line (e.g. using dosage in mg/unit as the intervention variable).

Rather than coding the intensity or the level of a design variable, you might be interested in using *state change* or *change rates* as the independent variable (e.g. registering relative increase/decrease in dosage over time). Conventional analysis models for metric data usually assume equally-spaced intervals between times of measurement, although some approaches can accommodate the irregular case. If you choose to depict/plot time series data before considering formal analyses (as you always should), ignoring the spacing issue is asking to be led astray. Therefore, it is recommended that not only logical time or design time (like measurement sequence t_1, t_2, . . ., T) be coded into a time series data structure, but that a chronological record (calendar time) is kept in addition.

Roughly, hypotheses for metric data split into two groups: (a) those conveying total series information (no data reduction performed) and (b) those operating on statistics for specific intervals. Hypotheses of the first group usually pertain to investigating the *time series structure* in that they aim at modeling serial dependency or fitting a functional form to the empirical series in order to predict future values. ARIMA-models or, more generally, state-space models and curve-fitting methods, respectively, are most useful for this purpose. Tests for *intervention hypotheses*, on the other hand, often collapse data from specific intervals of the total series into moment parameters for level, variability or latency and then perform tests on the differences in these parameters or on their covariation with design variables. In the most simple case, you would compare the baseline mean with a post-intervention mean of a criterion variable (see Figure 10.1). But, in later sections, you will find that serial dependency adds a lot of complication to statistical analysis and that classical methods are not be easily adopted to time series data. Now let's see what hypotheses can be devised for nonmetric data.

Discrete data occurs in many ways:

1. The response may be *dichotomous* by nature (presence/absence of a feature in a sequence of fixed time intervals). Time sampling leads to a binary time series. Your intervention may be aimed at achieving a permanent shift to the favorable state.
2. The response may be subject to *post-hoc dichotomization/ categorization*. You define a cut-off for any feature measured on an interval or ordinal scale level and assign a presence/success or absence/failure value to a secondary indicator or dummy variable. Common methods include mean/median splitting relative to the total observation period (client feels better/worse compared to his average rating) or temporal phasing (client feels better/worse than at a baseline assessment). You might also rely on an external reference like population norms to de-

fine a cut-off point. Your intervention goals correspond to the previous.

3. Any metric or discrete series may be transformed into a *change profile*. Suppose you have obtained a binary series using time sampling. Your primary interest is to determine the point of inflection (when do favorable responses overcome? or, stated differently, when do state changes occur less often? or, when do 'runs' of favorable responses become increasingly longer?). A common method to code change itself lies with assigning a zero to state preservation, -1 for transition from favorable to unfavorable state or $+1$ for the opposite. The same mechanics apply to time series of metric data. You can also use the sign of differences of successive responses to construct a change profile (e.g. '++—+—++++' for incremental learning curves). Your intervention may be aimed at reducing oscillation of states or at installing a stable trend in response.

4. The response are *event counts*. Your client might keep a diary for his daily headache seizures or the number of pain-free hours per week. Event sampling leads to frequency series. Your intervention may be aimed at approaching a continuing zero record for a criterion event.

5. The responses are *discrete waiting times*, e.g. the number of fixed-time intervals until occurrence of the next event (headache seizure) is recorded. Your intervention may be aimed at increasing or decreasing waiting times and may change/terminate when a criterion duration has been achieved.

Let us now try to map these omnibus types of hypotheses and some derivations to suitable statistical models.

10.3 GRAPHICAL DISPLAY OF SINGLE-CASE DATA

Before engaging in formal statistical analysis, it is always advisable to inspect the data visually and gain some preliminary understanding of your client's evolution. In the following, we discuss some basic issues in graphical analysis of both metric and categorical data. Evaluating relative merits of graphical versus statistical analysis of single-case data would be far beyond the scope of this chapter, and for further details the reader is referred to Kazdin (1984) and Franklin et al. (1996). In the case of metric data, it is usual to graph data across treatment conditions. Calendar time or therapy phase (as an independent variable) appears on the abscissa, and intensity measures of dependent variables appear on the ordinate. It is recommended, though, not to rely on 'eyeballing' the plot alone: while emphasizing the obvious, perception may discard the relevant. This holds true especially for high-variability data and data from complex designs (like multiple baseline or interaction plans). As with statistics, it is common to summarize or 'smooth' plotted data by taking phase means rather than raw data points, or by applying regression methods; spread-sheet applications like MS-Excel™ comprise curve-fitting modules that may be used to calculate and graphically display regression lines. It is usually a good idea to triple-overlay plots of raw data, overall regression line and phase-specific regression (e.g. baseline vs intervention trend) in order to evaluate treatment impact. Overlaying facilitates identification of outliers and may point to further time series characteristics that must be taken into account: confounding of trend and variability, nonlinearity, phase-specific trends that may or may not cancel out relative to overall trend, just to name a few. Figure 10.1 depicts four short series from a standard A-B-C design (baseline, intensive treatment, nontreatment, transfer phase). Consider subpanel (a): intense consideration of the problem in question and strong preoccupation may have caused heavy ups and downs in your client's measure of self-esteem while no final benefit could be achieved compared to the baseline level. As a consequence, fitting an overall regression results in a nearly flat line from pre- to post-test. On the other hand, we cannot readily say that treatment has shown no impact at all: increased variability in the treatment period may be due to an improvement in your client's ability of introspection and disclosure. In terms of experimentation, however, high variability within a phase, and worse, nonconstant variability over time within a phase, is assumed to be indicative of a lack of control.

Subpanel (b) illustrates a major pitfall of regression methods: Fitting an overall regression line and disregarding temporal structure (by using all data points) leads to the erroneous conclusion of an

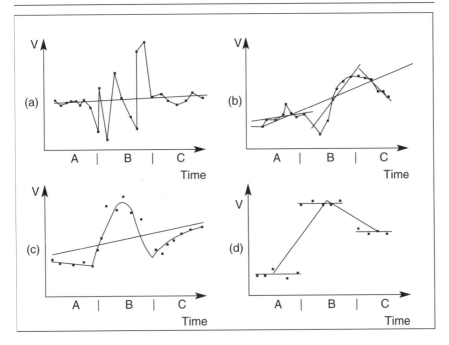

Figure 10.1   Short time series plots with regression lines superimposed

upward trend, indicating improvement. Fitting phase-specific curves reveals a strong positive impact of treatment after a near-constant baseline, but also suggests a downward trend after treatment completion. From these data, you might at best expect a return to the baseline level. Note that within-phase trends can be considered reasonably linear, which is not true at all for subpanel (c). Here, overall regression takes on the same form and clearly displays poor fit, but your conclusion of long-term benefit seems adequate even though your client returned to baseline level after treatment completion. In subpanel (d), mean level of response is almost identical to mean level in (c), but your conclusion is different: treatment has shifted your client's response by nearly a constant in the desired direction (homogeneous impact), completion of treatment diminished the effect by a constant backshift but still keeps responses significantly above baseline level. Note that, in subpanel (d), minimal variability within phases or small, homogeneous deviation of data points from regression lines are major points in interpreting the graph. Because regression lines are all flat and differ only by intercept, you can confine the analysis to evaluating the phase means. In analogy to standard ANOVA, you assume the presence of the 'effect' when 'between-variation' (differences of phase means from the time series mean or, more generally: change in level between phases) significantly outweighs 'within-variation' (deviation of data points from phase mean). Unfortunately, time series data usually exhibit features that do not allow for an ANOVA-style analysis (e.g. autocorrelation, see below). But in terms of visual inspection, examination of level and level-to-variance relations in different phases is still useful for receiving your first impression.

Parsonson and Baer (1978) describe heuristics by which to evaluate the treatment impact in single-case graphs. Generally, you will need a stable 'flat line' baseline in order to attribute the onset on trend in the intervention phase to your treatment. Other rules of thumb suggest that less overlap between measures of adjacent phases is associated with greater impact and that consistent patterns of trend or level/variability over similar intervention phases (replications) further support the notion of a treatment effect. Statisticians also recommend inspection of residual graphs in order to informally evaluate fit of trend/regression models. Plotting differences of raw data points and values predicted by regression (appearing on the ordinate) across time (appearing on the abscissa) is useful for detecting influential outliers and nonlinearity. Other types of residual graphs are discussed in Gilchrist (1984); you will, however, have to rely on statistical programming packages to benefit from more sophisticated model diagnostics.

Graphs for binary data may be event-based or duration-based. Consider subpanels (a) and (b) in Figure 10.2. You have registered whether or not your client suffered from headache seizure during therapy. Using event-sampling, you mark the occurrence of the event (seizure) directly on an axis for continuous time or discrete time bins. On the other hand, using time-sampling, you simply count how often the event occurred within fixed-length time intervals. This is highly preferred over event-sampling because intervals can be arranged to correspond to treatment phases, as in subpanel (b).

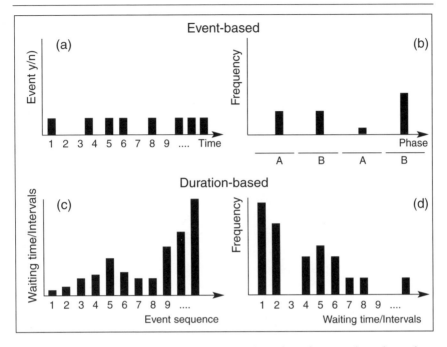

Figure 10.2   Binary time series plots: event-based vs duration-based graphs

As can easily be seen, event marker density in subpanel (a) translates to bar height (event count) in subpanel (b). A statistical test may then be used to trace possible trends and variability patterns of event probabilities over time sequences. Subpanels (c) and (d) are based on duration data, by marking waiting times between successive instantations of the event across time and depicting the frequency distribution of fixed-length waiting times in a histogram, respectively. A reduction in seizure counts corresponds to increasing waiting times in subpanel (c), with infinite waiting time being indicative of full remission (note that, naturally, this cannot be assessed within the time limits of therapy, and analysts speak of censored data because the observation period may end before the occurrence of the next event). In subpanel (d), positive outcome in terms of prolonged duration would cause the mode of the frequency distribution of waiting times to shift over time, progressively skewing the entire distribution from right to left. Therefore, generating the graph at the end of each treatment phase allows you to monitor your client's progress.

We realize that discrete data graphs are seldom found in clinical literature and may take time to get accustomed to, but there are benefits: they provide a straightforward inspection and monitoring tool for data types that are quite likely to emerge from processual assessment in controlled-practice settings, and they help to elucidate results from statistical tests. The latter also applies to graphs of metric data. Franklin et al. (1996) view visual inspection as being descriptive and mostly of heuristic use, and consider statistical analysis as being inferential and predictive in that it allows for probabilistic attributions of causality. Note that this is a conjecture rather than an assertion for various reasons that have been discussed intensively in methodology. It is agreed, however, that both strategies constitute complementary approaches to the evaluation of hypotheses and that graphical analysis is an indispensable tool in controlled-practice settings.

10.4   STATISTICAL ANALYSIS

Following our basic principle of not complicating things, we will not discuss the process of statistical modelling and testing in its own right or account for foundations like distribution theory and the concept of stochastic processes. We simply *deal* with them, and try to avoid what Clark (1963) defined as the 'error of the third kind', that is 'giving exact answers to the wrong questions' (p. 469). We proceed by providing you with a sort of matched 'hypothesis-to-test-given-scale-of-data' list. Therefore, in the following, we intend to (1) sensitize you for three major problems common to all data-driven inquiry, (2) define data scenarios for your setting, and (3) provide you with a set of analysis tools for these data.

Statistics for the single case: some caveats

Sampling

Sampling refers to the process of obtaining data points for a variable space—that is, selecting a number of clients, possibly assigning them to design conditions, and finally assessing them on criterion variables. It is understood that in a controlled-practice 'sampling framework' randomization or stratification methods cannot apply and the term 'sampling' receives a slightly different meaning. In our setting, only rarely will you be sampling clients from a larger population ('asking many instead of all'). Rather you will *sample in time*—that is, tracing a client's development by assessing repeated measures over several predefined occasions (available sample) while your therapy goes on (its duration defining the population of all possible time points). In rather fortunate circumstances you might even be able to parallel this sampling process with other clients of the same or similar indication and therapy. If there is not too much 'between-persons' variability present, you may at a later stage integrate cases in order to enhance your general conclusion (see below).

Either way, you will typically dispose of data from 1 to 10 cases (how many clients are participating?), measured on 2 to 30 occasions (how many recording sessions in a therapy?) on several variables (reflecting design and outcome parameters). If you review statistical literature for statistical models that account for this scenario, you are likely to find that good statistical advice is rare and that you are often better to resort to descriptive graphical analysis. The cardinal problem lies in the fact that 'real' statistics deal with real batches of data in that they rely on approximating certain theoretical *distributions*, and that 10 data points are hardly enough to bring about the shape of, say, a normal distribution or form a time series 'long' enough to estimate an autocorrelation parameter (see below). Note that this need not be a substantial problem since the data may in fact have been 'generated' by a process that 'would' have formed a regular normal curve once you obtained 'enough' data points. But in a controlled-practice 'sampling framework' you will seldom be in the position to raise this argument. Roughly speaking, in order to use standard statistical models legitimately you are supposed to have a 'sufficient' sample size (many independent cases, N) regardless of retest times (arbitrary T), or many, many retests of a single case (time series for serially correlated data: arbitrary N, big T), or both. Either way results in a set of data points of sufficient size to compute reliable estimates of parameters at an adequate level of *statistical power*. As a result, in controlled-practice settings, sampling limitations narrow down the set of sound statistical models, but we are prepared to present you with some techniques that are both sound and feasible.

But sampling problems do not reduce to mere sample size issues. Choosing the time between measurements (retest intervals) can seriously affect your conclusions. Consider the following cases:

- A variable may display a well-defined up-and-down pattern but you happened to assess it only on occasions when it had a value of '3'. Put differently: you *'undersampled'* the process because change occurred more quickly than your sampling frequency could trace it.
- A variable may display a near-constant linear trend of little variance but you happened to assess it when it contained many errors. In a classical test theory framework a manifest measure is defined as the sum of a true value and a random error component. In this paradigm, you sort of *'mis-sampled'* the process because you obtained outliers from a fairly flat line, and your data show some artifical pattern over time. The only recovery would be obtaining more data points.
- A variable displays slow change in time but you happened to choose too narrow retest intervals. You might miss the trend (slow component) over to much random variation. This *'oversampling'* poses no particular difficulties if you apply regression techniques, but may lead to an erroneous conclusion once you rely on visual inspection alone.

As a consequence, you will need prior knowledge from theory or experience of when, reasonably, to expect changes in a variable, and at which rate and magnitude. It is also important to account for the effect of different lengths in retest intervals, if measurement in equally spaced intervals is not feasible for practical reasons.

Missing values

Obtaining missing values and outliers is an almost inevitable phenomenon in every data collection. Considering poor sample sizes in our setting, missing values constitute a serious threat to statistical validity and may even render formal analyses impossible. Unfortunately, all remedies, like imputation methods, rely on 'enough' other complete data points in order to reliably estimate the missing candidate. Roughly, there are only two ways to proceed:

- Identify the nature of missing values: (1) are data *missing at random*, (2) do clients consistently deny response to certain variables (*missing by item*), do some clients consistently deny any response, or (3) does denial occur only in certain temporal phases (*missing by phase*)? From this, you might gain insight as regards limitations in your assessment instruments, homogeneity of clients or therapy effects on disclosure or compliance.
- Identify variables that differentiate completers from non-completers in order to adapt assessment to specific *response sets* in different types of clients.

Obviously, the best way to 'deal' with missing values is to have a generous allocation of subjects and measurement occasions, and avoid artificially compensating for 'natural' sample mortality.

Outliers

An *outlier* is a data point that lies 'outside' the data distribution, where 'outside' usually means some 2–3 units of standard deviation away from the mean (assuming metric data, similar concepts hold for polytoneous data [category overload]). Still, we feel that a mere statistical definition may be too narrow, since you should always consider that there is a conceptual difference between *'outliers'* and *'extreme values'*. The latter in fact belong to the 'main set' (every continuous distribution has long tails, remember, so these cases might just lie on the *'far side'* rather than the *'outside'*). Outliers, on the other hand, are additionally defined on grounds of conceptual reasons. One of these reasons is sample homogeneity. Suppose that a subject displays an 'outlying' value on just one variable, but is clearly 'in-group' with respect to 20 other variables (that is, he shares the common range of values). We would readily agree that the deviant comes indeed from the same population and might have happened to misunderstand instructions for that item. If, on the other hand, deviations of similar extent were present in variables that highly correlate with the variable in question, the subject then shows consistency with respect to an underlying construct and should be considered to have a 'true' extreme value on the variable. Now suppose he had deviant values on many correlated and uncorrelated variables. You might then check whether this subject was misdiagnosed in the first place and does not belong to the sample (he is *'out-sample'* rather than outlier).

Extreme values and outliers do not threaten feasibility but they affect the performance of statistical tests in that 'true' values of statistical functions such as means, regression slopes or significance probabilities may be grossly over- or underestimated in their presence. A crucial question in statistics has always been whether or not to exclude data points from subsequent statistical analyses. We propose that extreme values be always kept in the data set no matter how great their influence on statistical tests, since they are valid values and we cannot legitimately cut down the sample to fit our needs in empirical research. However, outliers, when properly defined and identified, *should* be excluded from analysis since they are 'mis'-sampled by item or by test and distort inference to a population to which they do not belong. Note that you should consider only a 'few' outliers: if some cases deviate overduly from the 'regular' mass and/or if graphs reveal homogeneous clusters of such subjects, they should not be conceived as outliers but should form a separate subsample. It is your turn, then, to identify moderating variables that differentiate these cases systematically from others. In such cases, outliers do not stem from random error influences but carry information and need special attention (perhaps both in the statistical and clinical sense).

We regret having possibly discouraged the use of statistics, but there is in fact little you can do when faced with small samples *and* missing values *and* outliers (that lead to missing variable values when they are excluded). The best we can say is that, generally, you should use statistics to back up (or revise) conclusions drawn from experience or graphical analyses when requirements are met, and that you should strictly refrain from using them otherwise. *Clearly, it is the second point that deserves more attention.* Note that we are making a strictly technical point here: whether statistical analysis is an appropriate approach at all is quite another issue.

Tests for metric data

Before we proceed to the core of statistical tests we need to define some scenarios of data collection. We must then try to associate the resulting *data structures* with appropriate *statistical tests* that reflect the nature of your different *hypotheses* (see section 10.2). These are the basic dimensions for choosing a technique for analysis.

Scenarios for data collections

Scenario A: Small groups and moderate replication. You have collected data for 10 (or more) individuals on several outcome parameters at 2 (or more) measurement occasions in time ($N_{10+}T_{2+}$). Possibly, you may discern distinct treatment phases over time, with a two-point *pre-post comparison* being the simplest case. Your sample constitutes a group, and your further arguments pertain to *group statistics* like the mean or median. You expect a *shift in location over time*; that is, a trend. Fortunate enough, you may be able to introduce another, independent group of clients into the design and hypothesize that groups show a different pre-post evolution. Note that this *interaction of a between-groups (or treatment) factor and time* matches the classical definition of an *effect* as outlined in Cook and Campbell (1979). We restrict these kinds of analyses to a base of 10 or more cases for reasons of statistical theory. In order to use standard tests that assume normality and homogeneity of variances, like *t*-tests for example, you should have at least 30 cases or more. Certain 'nonparametric' tests may operate on at least 10 cases. Fewer cases clearly point to the next scenario.

Scenario B: Single-case and high replication. You dispose of data of a *single case* but you were able to assess the variables of interest some 30 times (or more, N_1T_{30+}). Your primary interest lies with the nature of your client's development (*change-in-structure*: straight trend versus cyclicity, latency and persistency of response to interventions, etc.; *change-in-slope*: at what rate does behavior change occur?) as well as with *change-in-level* of outcome parameters. You might try to associate eyeballed *structural breaks* in the graph of your data with temporal characteristics in your therapy plan ('onset of confrontation techniques led to abrupt decay in compliance that took some sessions to reinstall'). You use formal statistics to identify a *time series model* that closely parallels your data and further funds your intervention effect. In other cases, you might be interested in *predicting* future evolution rather than in *testing* for pre-post differences. Again, we restrict these kinds of analyses to a base of 30 or more data points in time for reasons of statistical theory: whether you assess the nature of serial dependency in a time series or simply compare baseline to post-intervention level, either way you will need this sample size in order to reliably estimate associated statistical parameters like autocorrelation, etc. Note that 30 replications are regarded as the indisputable minimum for a special case application of already restricted statistical validity. Sometimes even greater loads of data automatically fall into place from self-monitoring devices (e.g. your client is expected to keep a diary on headache seizures).

Methods for small groups and moderate replication (scenario A)

Methods for analyzing data from this scenario comprise classical parametric tests like the *t*-test for matched pairs (two measurement occasions in one group) or the *F*-test (two or more measurement occasions in one group or more) as typically applied in Analysis of Variance (ANOVA). Here, we enter the realm of *multiple group comparisons* (Waldmann & Petermann, 1998), with groups being rather small in a controlled-practice setting.

Basically, in ANOVA-style analyses, you devise the null hypothesis that means are equal in all groups across the levels of an experimental factor. In the case of one group assessed at several occasions, the factor would be 'time', and the actual cases in groups would be the same subjects. Thus, put in terms of repeated measures, the null hypothesis states that no change took place in either direction. Since the usual assumption of independence of subjects across factor levels is most unlikely to hold with a repeated measurement factor, special techniques to assess the impact of serial correlation and compensate for its effects on the mechanics of the significance test have been devised (see Huynh & Feldt, 1970, for details). If you succeed in rejecting the null hypothesis—that is, you observe a significant probability value of the *F*-test in your analysis printout—you conclude that *samples differ* and 'something' must have 'caused' the difference. Stop for a minute and pay attention to the quoted items in the former sentence since the notion of inferring causality from a significant statistical test is generally false, no matter how frequently it is stated explicitly or (more often) implicitly. What can be inferred from such tests is highly disputed among methodologists and we hesitate to even summarize the debate (however, you may take a look at Waldmann, 1997). Also note that this 'something' cannot be identified by proper logic if you fail to have a strict parallel control group and cannot test for differential change.

Differential change occurs when one group displays a change in a variable from pre-test to post-test (more generally: over time) while another, independent sample does not, or drifts in the other direction. Suppose you applied some treatment to one sample while some other clients constitute a waiting control group. Prior to intervention, you assess both groups and assign clients to either group in a way that assures pre-test equivalence on the outcome parameter of interest. You would be inclined to attribute a statistically significant reduction in, say, cigarettes smoked during your treatment in the case where your untreated clients maintain a smoking behavior common to both groups as a pre-test offset. Stated differently, you will need to implement a *control group design with repeated measures* to come close at least to what is meant by a causal effect. Cook and Campbell (1979) discuss various research designs and corresponding models for analysis as well as their relative merits in attaining causal assertions.

Methods that operate with sample sizes below the recommended 30 or more, as typically required for ANOVA-style tests, comprise the Wilcoxon Test (one group pre-post) and Friedman's 'ANOVA for ranks' (one group multiple occasions) to name the most powerful. Note that these tests have not been devised for small samples but are equally applicable to small-sample problems as they relax certain assumptions from statistical theory that are very unlikely to be met in a 'from-ten-cases-on' scenario of data collection. Also, they do not test exactly the same hypotheses as an ANOVA-style test but still pertain to inference about *shifts in central tendencies over time*. Refer to Hays (1970) to learn more about the internal machinery of these nonparametric tests that rely on relative ranks of subjects instead of the measurement values themselves, and may thus be preferred over ANOVA even in large samples whenever metric scale properties must be doubted for some reason. In order to analyze ranks, measures at *ordinal level* are still required. But directional assertions like 'feeling much better today' might be more adequate and reliable than differences on a metric (interval) scale, anyway.

Methods for a single case and moderate-to-high replication (senario B)

We now turn to statistical models for the most likely situation in your controlled-practice setting. These methods fall into two categories, roughly: (1) adoptions of the above, classical test that try to integrate or circumvent the effects of serially correlated data, and (2) models that explicitly focus on the structure of serial dependency and conceive the data as a time series. Methods in the first category primarily address the issue of *change in level* and require moderate replication rates (less than 30–50 data points over time), while methods in the second assess *change in slope and in structure* and ususally do not operate reliably below the 'more-than-30–50-measures' level. Sample sizes that intersect these limits (30–50) may be appropriate for both types of analyses when certain criteria are met. In the following we will base our discussion on data sets that are similar to those depicted in Figure 10.1: a single variable has been measured over time, while different levels have been defined for the time factor that corresponds to treatment phases (see interval markers on the time axes in Figure 10.1).

Adoption of classical tests for time series data. Every psychologist or psychiatrist supposedly has received some training in statistical methods, and it seems appealing to examine the extent to which well-known techniques like *t*- or *F*-test-based methods may be adopted for a time series analysis. If you check the enormous body of literature on this issue, you are likely to find that there is a general problem common to all statistical options within the adoption rationale: *autocorrelation*. Thus, in the following, we need to define the concept of autocorrelation and evaluate its impact on standard tests. Roughly speaking, there are two categories of methods in this framework: those that natively incorporate auto-correlation and those that circumvent the problem by using robust tests.

First, we need to define autocorrelation. It results from correlating a series of data points assessed from the same individual over time with the same data series from the same individual lagged ahead in time. A first-order *lagged* series is created by simply shifting the original series one time period ahead into a new time series. If you compute a standard Pearson correlation coefficient for these two series, the first observation in the original series is paired with the first shifted one (that is: the observation at $t + 1$ with respect to time ordering in the original series). Put differently: each obser-vation in the 'new' series is matched to the one that preceded it in time. The same principle of stepwise lag displacement applies to higher order autocorrelation coefficients. For a series of length T there are $T - 1$ autocorrelation coefficients, but since every shift cuts off one data point from the new series there are practical limitations to the calculation. In most cases, autocorrelations quickly decrease in magnitude (and statistical significance) as the lag (shift width) increases. You would also expect this fade-out to occur for conceptual reasons, since the influence of data points 'further away in the past' are likely to exert less influence on actual data point than data points closer to it.

Now, there is a good and a bad thing about autocorrelation. A benefit from autocorrelation is that it may be taken for a measure of *serial dependency*: it represents the degree to which the actual value can be predicted from preceding values, with autocorrela-tion *order* indicating how many steps back in the time series one should use for this prediction. Positive first-order autocorrelation indicate trend, whereas negative first-order coefficients point to rapid oscillations (a high value is succeeded immediately by a low value and vice versa). It seems obvious that models of the second category do not only account for, but in fact rely on, autocorrelation.

The bad thing about autocorrelation is that it distorts the mecha-nisms of standard testing models like the *t*-test since one can no longer assume independence of error terms and, as a consequence, test statistics like F and t are seriously affected. Depending upon the sign of autocorrelation, standard errors in standard regression analyses or ANOVA-style tests for differences will be inflated or deflated, resulting in test statistics—and thus p-values—either too big or too small. Here, autocorrelation possibly entails misleading conclusions (Huynh & Feldt, 1970). Put differently, *these models are not 'robust' against violating an assumption that is likely to be violated by the very nature of your time-series design*. It turns out that you should always at least *check for* autocorrelation before analyzing single-subject time-series data by whatever modeling procedure. Most spreadsheet programs allow for computation of autocorrelation coefficients. We suggest that you might use these procedures to determine the magnitude of serial dependency. If it is not significant, you are perfectly entitled to proceed the standard way and perform a t-test or the like. Kazdin (1984) gives a detailed worked example of a t-test used to evaluate statistical significance of a difference in phase means when no autocorrelation is present in neither phase. Otherwise we will have to look for alternatives when we are interested in aggregate change-in-level analyses.

Note that 'aggregate' means that we are willing to collapse multiple data points within a time period (an intervention phase, say) into a *statistic* like the mean of that phase. Of course, we lose information by doing so, but why run complicated analyses that account for any data point and serial dependency when all you want to know is whether there has been a substantial increase in overall level of a variable from baseline to post-test period. Figure 10.1 subpanel (d) depicts a case for which this strategy is appropriate. A serious counterargument, however, states that you will completely miss the point in cases where an upward trend is present in the baseline phase, and a downward trend in the post-intervention phase. Then, means might be just the same while your client's behavior improved and then faded away back to baseline level. This is why we urged you to *always* let graphical analysis precede statistical testing.

Gorman and Allison (1996) discuss the use of *randomization tests* that dispense with some rather restrictive assumptions of ANOVA-style tests while preserving the general idea of testing for differences in subsamples defined by partitioning data points on a time axis. Kazdin (1984) illustrates the rationale of such tests by a worked example and comments on practical restrictions. Revusky (1967) contributed to the analysis of short time series by devising *a Rn-Test-of-Ranks*. This may be employed to detect intervention effects in multiple baseline designs (quite common in research on behavior-oriented therapy) and relies on ranking responses at the point of intervention for several clients. Note that, statistically speaking, both the randomization test and the Revusky R*n* are based on a random assigment of subjects or baselines to treatment onset in time, a prerequisite that may seriously conflict with individual client's needs in your actual setting.

Another means of analysis that is particularly useful for clinical practice settings is the so-called *split-middle technique* devised by White (1972, 1974): which (a) combines graphical display and formal statistical inference, (b) applies to single subject data as well as to groups, and (c) actually fits any design that divides the time line into different phases of the therapy process. Although it *resembles* regression analysis by fitting a straight line to data points within phases, it uses completely different construction rules for this purpose that render it a descriptive technique in the first place. The procedure is sensitive to change in level as well as to change in slope. Several lines for different phases may then be compared on a statistical basis using a simple binomial test that doesn't concern autocorrelation.

The primary parameter of the split middle method is a rate of behavior change over time—that is, the frequency of any target behavior is recorded over therapy sessions (ordinate) and is plotted against session number on the abscissa (time axis) within each phase of the total therapy process. A linear trend line is estimated within each phase following a construction rule that relies entirely on ranking data points for obtaining the median relative to ordinate and abscissa within each half of each phase (hence the term 'split middle'). This may sound complicated, but is in fact quite easily accomplished for a given printout of the plot and involves no computations. Kazdin (1984) provides a worked example for this trend line construction. Given a fitted trend line, its slope may be expressed numerically. The level within a phase depends on whether it will be evaluated against the subsequent phase (in which case it is defined by the behavior rate recorded at the phase's last session) or against the previous phase (first session's value). Dividing levels and slopes from consecutive phases results in a phase-by-phase measure of change in level and slope that summarizes the progress of the therapy with respect to different phases. Now suppose you extend a baseline trend into an intervention phase (baseline projection). Since this 'within intervention phase' trend line has been constructed to divide the data points of that phase into an upper and a lower half (again: 'split-middle'), you should expect this line to be displaced well above the extrapolated baseline trend (increase of behavior rate being the intervention goal, of course). Put differently, *the baseline trend extension is not a valid estimate of the intervention phase trend when there is a substantial intervention effect.* In this case, the baseline trend cannot separate the upper and lower data points as it did in the pre-intervention phase on behalf of the construction rule. Again, put differently: a data point's chance of falling above the projected baseline trend is $p = 0.5$, given the null hypothesis of no change across phases. A binomial test, then, shows whether the probability of obtaining the actual or greater number of data points in the intervention above the projected line is small enough to reject this null hypothesis.

We realize that this technique has not been used extensively in the past (maybe because it does not involve computation heavy enough to warrant scientific attention), but we advocate its use for three major reasons. Perhaps the most relevant benefit from this technique lies in the facts that (1) it does not reduce the entire data set of a phase into a mean but works on level, slope and on changes in both; (2) Kazdin (1984) sees an 'important applied significance' of the split middle method, since 'if the data suggest that behavior is not changing at a sufficient rate to obtain a particular goal, the intervention can be altered' (p. 318); and (3) taking further into account that you regularly dispose of the type of graph required for this method by means of your documentation system (described in previous sections), *running a 'split middle chart-and-test' procedure might be a reasonable 'analytic companion' to your therapy monitoring and planning.*

Time series analysis and tests for structural breaks. From the previous section you know that any data assessed over time from the same individual constitutes a time series. As a technical term, time series analysis has a more specialized meaning and refers to a family of models first propagated by Box and Jenkins (1970): ARIMA models. ARIMA is an acronym for *Autoregressive Integrated Moving Average*, and, *technically*, the method is just as complex as the name suggests. The basic principles, however, are straightforward. You have a rather long ($T > 50$, 100 recommend: the more the better) time series. A plot reveals that, as a whole, the series displays a slight upward trend. If you eyeball it fast enough from left to right, you might even register a sine-like wave in addition. You will certainly take note of lots of fast-varying ups and downs and peaks that seem to occur at no special rule. Here you go: you have just separated the three main components of any time series: *trend*, cyclicity (or *seasonality*) and random *noise*. ARIMA models do just the same by devising an additive model of these three components, with a focus on the last one. Trend is subtracted from the original series by taking *differences* of successive data points. What's left is a confounded mixture of a regular seasonal and a stochastic component. Note that 'stochastic' does not mean 'by chance' or 'at random'. It means: not deterministic, and not easily described. ARIMA techniques try to fit an additive, linear, and regression-style model to what is left from the original data when fully predictable trend and seasonality have been extracted. As you know from standard statistics, regression methods do not fully predict another variable: there is an error term (hence: stochastic, to finish vocabulary). ARIMA models use past (or lagged) values from the de-trended series or past noise components ('chance shocks') to predict the actual value. The first idea corresponds roughly to *autoregression*, and you already suspect that ARIMA will make use of autocorrelation coefficents to estimate the regression equation. The second idea seems rather difficult to understand: how to predict a value from past residuals. Technically, this part makes up the *moving average* component. As we noted earlier, we will not bother you with details on this methods. What you get as a result is some equation that allows you to predict future values to some extent and that quantifies the influence of past values on the actual one, thereby offering a measure of serial dependency. While ARIMA models have received major recognition as a means of *structural modeling* and prognosis, they seem to be of limited value for therapeutical practice. Add their computational complexity and the wide variety of submodels and derivations, and you can understand why we do not recommend them for controlled-practice settings. Since almost every textbook for statistics for time series data offers a section on ARIMA we felt that we should at least mention it.

We conclude by citing Kazdin (1984) who summarizes his reservations against ARIMA-style time series analysis using a fairly pragmatistic argument: 'The tests are complex and involve multiple steps that are not easily described in terms familiar to most researchers. For example, serial dependency and autocorrelation, two of the less esoteric notions underlying time series analysis, are not part of the usual training of researchers who conduct group studies in social sciences' (p. 302). No need to say, that you will need statistical software packages to actually perform these test. If you have one available *and* you are strongly convinced that your data might meet with ARIMA requirements *and* that results will be worth the effort, you might want to check the following references for the specialties indicated in brackets: Box, Jenkins and Reinsel (1994) [second edition by the originators of the method], Chatfield (1980) [integrated reader on time series analysis], Crosbie (1993) [short time series applications], Farnum and Stanton (1989) [forecasting], Gottman (1981) [ARIMA and extensions], McDowall et al. (1980) [Intervention analyses and transfer functions].

Tests for discrete data

In this final 'statistics' section, we will deal with binary time series corresponding to data types and hypotheses 1–3 in section 10.2. There are two ways, roughly, of analyzing such data, just as was case for metric data: considering the 'chain of events' as recorded, or collapsing it into event count parameters for predefined time intervals. The latter approach allows for the application of standard chi-square tests. You might split the time axis at the point of time of intervention onset and count your ones and zeros in both phases. Then, you organize the counts into a table (column dimension: baseline [0/1], row dimension: post-intervention [0/1]) and perform a regular Pearson's chi-square test to estimate an effect size. Please refer to virtually any textbook for statistics and details on chi-square mechanics. But there are some more sophisticated solutions in the line of the first-mentioned approach.

Recapturing data structures from section 10.2, either you have recorded the presence ('1') or absence ('0') of a specific event or phenomenon ('client did/did not attend the session', 'client was/ was not able to disclose intimate problems') or have post-hoc dichotomized your own rating ('client improved his ability of disclosure (yes/no)'). Your treatment is aimed at procuring a target pattern of events in time, like 'good communication skills displayed: Yes (1)' or 'relapse into drug consumption (0)'. You would attribute a permanent shift to the favorable state attributable to your treatment. If there was no treatment effect, you would expect instantation of favorable states or events by chance, or, in other words, in random order with respect to the whole record. This is precisely the null hypotheses for tests of *sequential nonrandomness*. There are several variations of these tests, depending on what you define as 'pattern' (as opposed to 'random' or 'chance variation') and whether you consider event counts or the number of fixed-length interval between events (time/event sampling, please return to section 10.2 for details, and re-examine Figure 10.2 in section 10.3 before continuing). Notions of sequential nonrandomness can be found in the following questions:

- Are *events distributed evenly or at random over all intervals* of assessment, or is there a **'rule'** (occupation test, David, 1950)? Essentially the same question is asked by the perhaps more familar 'runs' test (Stevens, 1939). Wallis and Moore (1941) have devised a similar test for data coded as a change profile (runs up, runs down, see section 10.2). When sequential randomness is present, you might even ask *which intervals carry an increased event probability* and compare the result to your session record.
- Do **event counts** *increase/decrease linearly over time* (Pfanzagl, 1994)? Here, the notion of 'rule' is specified as linear **trend** in aggregate data (counts of events in fixed-length intervals. Wallis

and Moore (1941) also offer a test for a monotonous trend in binary time series data. A term that you might come across in textbooks and which usually indicates trend in time series is *nonstationarity*.

- A similar, but slightly different question, however, asks whether *event probabilities are and remain constant over time* or do they follow a linear trend (Meyer-Bahlburg, 1969)?
- If there is sequential nonrandomness in a binary time series, at which point in time does trend begin? In other words: can a *point of inflection be determined* (Cochran, 1954)?
- Does the number of fixed-length time intervals between successive events increase/decrease, or *do events occur at increasing/ decreasing rate* (occur more often/more seldom)?

Bortz and Lienert (1998) provide excellent worked examples for most of these tests, with computations carried out 'by hand' in order to demonstrate the practical feasibility of these methods. Be assured that there are lots of highly sophisticated methods of an almost evil complexity available for analyzing discrete time series, most of which are not even implemented in major statistical packages, like SAS. As a consequence, and with reasonable methods readily at hand, we draw the same conclusion as we did at the end of the previous section: First graph your data using charts like those displayed in Figure 10.2, then apply a chi-square test where possible, using the methods indicated above to refine the analysis for more specialized hypotheses.

Post-processing results: Integration of single cases

Sometimes you cannot use all the data from different subjects at once and input all cases to any one of the above-mentioned methods for groups, because the sample size is too small or perhaps the subjects are so genuinely different that they should be considered as individual cases. For issues of therapy planning and monitoring of goal attainment, you need to draw conclusions from single-case analysis. Nevertheless, all subjects may have been exposed to the same treatment, and it seems reasonable to evaluate treatment effects by combining evidence from separate, but similar analyses. Stated differently: you are to perform meta-analysis in order to make inferences from samples (cases) to a population of all potential cases eligible for this treatment. A very simple method lies with applying a binomial test: let n be the number of subjects showing the effect out of N subjects treated, and let p be the error probability of each test (i.e. the conventional significance level $p = 0.05$). Insert these values into

$$p \text{ (combined)} = \sum_{n}^{N} \begin{bmatrix} N \\ n \end{bmatrix} p^n (1-p)^{(N-n)}$$

to obtain the combined significance probability (see Bortz and Lienert, 1998, for details). If the value does not exceed 0.05, the rejection of the null hypothesis is justified, taking all analyses into account simultaneously. If N individual analyses gave z-values as a result, then you obtain a combined chi-square test by simply letting $\chi^2 = \sum z^2$ with $df = N-1$ (Pearson Agglutination, see Lautsch and Lienert, 1993). Note that the binomial method applies to any primary analysis since any data structure and quality can be 'downsized' to the binomial level: you simply count who's hot and who's not. More sophisticated methods for combining results from different analyses can be found in Wolf (1980) as well as in Rosenthal (1991). As can be seen from these examples, computations can easily be carried out manually.

A word about software

Even though you could, you would not regularly *want* to perform data analyses this way. On the other hand, not many therapists would happily agree to buy, run, and maintain one of the major statistical programming packages like SAS™ or SPSS™. But there is a compromise: spreadsheet programs have become popular for their ease of use and their wide range of applications in both science and business. Microsoft Excel™ provides a variety of statistical functions (sample descriptives like mean, variance, sum and sum of squares, frequencies, correlations, etc.), predefined test routines (including t-test, chi-square and binomial test) and generators for values and probabilities from various distributions. Users need not make use of its powerful macro language to carry out computations but may simply insert formulas themselves into another column of the data sheet to produce immediate results. If new data are entered, results are automatically updated—a feature that facilitates data monitoring. Since Excel is integrated in a multicomponent office software suite, it is very easy to paste tables, results and graphs into the word processor and produce refined reports. Other office suites like Works™, StarOffice™ or Lotus 1-2-3™ provide similar functionality. It has become quite common for computers to be shipped with some integrated office suite pre-installed and ready for use, so their is a good chance that you will have the means available as a part of your office administration facilities. Should the need arise for more complex analyses, you might want to contact a CRO (contract research organisation) or seek collaboration with academic staff. Most medical schools or statistics departments offer consulting services to non-university health care providers.

Chapter 11

A DOCUMENTATION SYSTEM FOR CONTROLLED PRACTICE

11.1 DOCUMENTATION SYSTEM FOR CONTROLLED PRACTICE

The documentation of the pivotal factors of therapy and of single-case analysis is a distinctive part of controlled practice and a framework for documentation is presented in this chapter. Carrying out a single-case analysis according to controlled practice soon accumulates a large quantity of data such as feedback reports, files, and materials, and the documentation system eventually provides a data storage system that is supportive for the therapist. Without such a system data cannot be allocated for evaluation purposes. The closer a therapist follows the procedure suggested, the greater comparability is achieved, and the sooner will the therapist be able to learn from a comparison of single cases. First, however, data collection must display the following qualities:

- the database must be *unambiguous*
- single cases must be *comparable*
- the data set must be *complete* and
- the data collection must be *comprehensible*.

To fulfill these requirements the therapist should follow the suggestions provided in the sections referring to the use of documentation sheets (section 11.2) and electronic documentation (section 11.3). Then, the documentation system serves the following needs:

- extensive documentation of therapy
- basis for comprehensive evaluation, and
- storage system.

Here, evaluation is defined as a comparison of several therapies (cf. section 11.4). First, a summary is given of the parts of the documentation system. To this end we now insert documentation slots into Figure 3.2 , giving Figure 11.1.

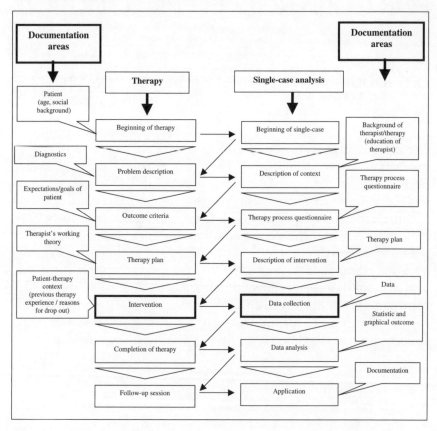

Figure 11.1   Documentation areas of therapy and the single-case analysis

Figure 11.1 lists 11 documentation areas altogether which describe the different steps of therapy and single-case analysis. Documentary information is collected on different documentation sheets, e.g. in the form of questionnaires. Based on the 11 documentation areas, 12 sheet are developed. This is illustrated in Figure 11.2.

Some of the data for documentation can be obtained from paperwork done during therapy:

- Documentation sheet No. 2: Graphical problem description
- Documentation sheet No. 3: Therapy process questionnaire, containing actual condition (AC) and specified conditions (SC) of the patient
- Documentation sheet No. 4: Development of questions from graphical treatment description
- Documentation sheet No. 5: Graphical treatment explanation
- Documentation sheet No. 8: Tabular therapy plan
- Documentation sheet No. 11: Therapy process graph. (Rules for the creation of the graph are described later.)

The overview in Figure 11.2 may be used as a *checklist* (documentation sheet No. 12) and helps to control the documentation system as a whole. The remaining documentation sheets are explained in the following section.

11.2   SUPPLEMENTARY INFORMATION

Some standardized documentation sheets which have not been explicitly listed before are presented now.

Preliminary note to guarantee anonymity. Inevitably the documentation system includes personal data. To protect this information from abuse and to interrelate it properly, all 11 documentation sheets should have the *same number* (key code or ID code). This number enables the user to relate each piece of information to the others.

Preliminary note to electronic storage. All the following documentation sheets contain notes on how data are electronically recorded in spreadsheets. The data of patient and therapist should be entered in spreadsheets in order to be able to evaluate recorded

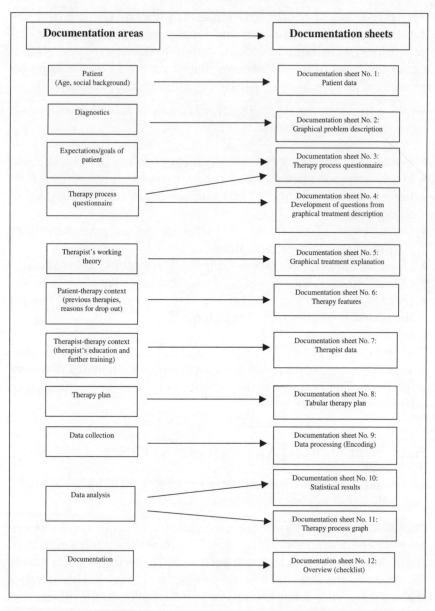

Figure 11.2 Matching of documentation areas and documentation sheets

therapies more easily. Therefore, it is necessary to provide both variable names and values for the spreadsheets; these are already listed in documentation sheets 1, 6, 7, 9 and 10. Answers to open format questions such as the question of nationality are keyed in as 'string' variables in the answer fields provided. How these spreadsheets are formed is described in section 11.3.

Documentation sheet No. 1: Patient data. In this sheet, socio-demographic data such as age, sex and marital status of the patient are recorded. These patient features are needed for later evaluation in order to form homogeneous groups of patients for meta-analysis. As a rule, the informed consent of the patient (cf. Box 5.1) is needed. An example of a patient documentation sheet is presented in Box 11.1.

Documentation sheet No. 6: Therapy features. This sheet contains information about the current therapy and previous attempts (cf. Box 11.2).

Documentation sheet No. 7: Therapist data. This sheet contains data pertaining to the therapist and the setting. The focus is on general, not-patient-specific basic conditions that give information on the most important parts of the background of the therapy. They complete the patient-specific description of the therapy plan (cf. Box 11.3). Of course these details do not have to be filled out for every patient; they are used only for evaluation.

Documentation sheet No. 9: Data processing. This sheet forms part of the evaluation documentation (cf. section 11.4). It contains details on data collection, such as sample size, the interval between measurements, and notes on missing data. These items of the therapy process questionnaire are encoded as 'var__1' to 'var__n'.

Remark. All data-processing steps should be documented. This should be a decisive criterion in choosing the evaluation software, since menu-driven use of a program is common but not easily comprehensible to others. Some programs have a so-called 'protocol option', where processing steps are output to a separate file.

Documentation sheet No. 10: Statistical results. The result presentation is composed of the statistical result sheet (No. 10) and the therapy process sheet (No. 11). It gives information about the

Box 11.1   Documentation sheet No. 1: Patient data
(including notes for variable names, e.g. (sex) and codes, e.g. male = (1))

(p_code)	**Patient code (ID code):**	_____	
(birth)	**Date of birth:**	_____	
p_sex)	**Sex:**	Male (1)	Female (2)
(nation)	**Nationality:**	_____	
(ethno)	**Ethnic group or race:**	_____	

Family

(family)	*Current marital status:*	Married (1)	Living in a partnership (2)
		Divorced (3)	Married, but separated from spouse (4)
		Single (5)	Widowed (6)
(children)	Children (number):	_____	
(siblings)	Siblings (number):	_____	
(finance)	*Situation:*	Secure (1)	Insecure (2)

Professional financial situation

(job)	Employment:	Durable (1)	Limited (2) None (3)
(ill)	Sick and being off work:	Yes (1)	No (2)
(illdays)	Sick days of the last 12 months:	_____	
(job_load)	Work load:	Full time (1)	Part time (2)
		On-demand/ negotiated (3)	Multiple load (4)
(educatio)	*Education:*	No school education (1)	High School (2)
		College (3)	Graduate School (4)
(home)	*Living situation:*	alone (1)	With partner and child/ren (2)
		With partner (3)	Single with child/ren (4)
		With parents (5)	With friends (6)
(agree)	*Consent to general evaluation:*	Yes (1)	No (2)

Box 11.2   Documentation sheet No. 6: Therapy features
(including notes for variable names, e.g. (sex) and codes, e.g. male = (1))

(p_code) **Patient code (ID code):**   _____

Previous therapies of patient:
(t_acco) Number of previous therapies: _____
(t_break) Number of drop outs: _____
(b_reason) Reasons for drop out: _____

Present therapy
          Therapy duration:
(t-Begin) Beginning: Month/year_____ – (t-end) End: Month/year_____
(freqenc) Session frequency (average per month):   _____
(interrup) Intermissions: _____ in weeks
(ending) Termination type: Regular (1) Attrition (2)

(end_c) Reason for completion:
          Patient sees no need for therapy   Therapist sees no need for
          any more (1)   therapy any more (2)
          Patient recognizes deterioration (3) Therapist recognizes deterioration (4)
          Missing funding (5)   Referral (6)
          Not named (7)

(t_single) Single (1)   Group therapy (2)
(t_finance) Financing: Patient himself (1) Insurance (2) Other funding sources (3)

Therapeutic assistance
(supervis) Regular supervision?   Yes (1)   No (2)
(consult) Consultation with other colleagues: Yes (1)   No (2)
(allianz) Therapy alliances with other occupational groups:
          None (0)   Physicians (1) Psychologist (2)
          Psychiatrist (3)   Nurse (4)   Physiotherapist (5)
          Occupational therapist (6) Family (7)   Further reference persons, e.g.
                                                     (friends) (8)
          Community nurse (9)   Juridical (10)

(material) Therapy material:

          _____

          _____

          _____

Box 11.3   Documentation sheet No.7: Therapist data
(including notes about variable names, e.g. (t_sex) and codes,
e.g. male = (1))

Therapist features

(t_code)   Code: _____

(t_age)   Age: _____

(t_experi)   Job experience as a therapist in whole years: _____

(t_sex)   Sex: Male (1)   Female (2)

(t_educa)   Therapy education:

Behavioral therapy (1)	Cognitive behavioral therapy (2)
Cognitive therapy (3)	Analytic therapy (4)
Client-centered therapy to Rogers (5)	Rational-emotive therapy to Ellis (6)
Gestalt therapy (7)	Physically based therapy (e.g. bioenergetics) (8)
Neurological-oriented therapy (9)	Psychopharmacological therapy (10)
Biological therapies (11)	Transactional analysis (12)
Musicotherapy (13)	Other orientation (15)

(t_adds)   *Additional orientation or education:*_____

Setting

(inout)   Outpatient (1)   Inpatient (2)   Both (3)

(setting)   Place: Therapy room (1)
                                       At home/at work or real-life setting (2)
                                       Controlled setting (3)

(institut)   Institution: _____

(organi)   Organization: _____

Box 11.4   Documentation sheet No 9: Data processing

Patient code (ID code): _____

(q_freq)   Number of the surveys altogether: _____

(q_mis)   Number of missing surveys

(distan)   Interval between surveys: _____ in days

(software)   Used software: _____

(version)   Version: _____

Did you check for incorrect data?   Yes (1)   No (2)

(imputat1. . . 9)   Was missing data being replaced?

  • No substitution (0)

  • Retrospective addition by the patient (1)

  • Mean average value (2)

  • Smoothing average (3)

  • Other (4)

Variable transformations

(transf1 . . . 9)   Which: _____

(How1 . . . 9)   How: _____

(New_var1 . . . 9) New variable: _____

(Content1 . . . 9) Content of the new variable: _____

---

statistical tests carried out and lists the analysis software (see Box 11.5). If the interpretations of the therapy process graphics are not statistically evaluated, this must be so indicated.

Documentation sheet No. 11: Therapy process graphs. Based on the process graphs, one can get a fast impression on whether single symptoms have improved. In order to prevent graphs of different processes to vary to much, some rules (cf. Box 11.6) are introduced. These rules standardize process graphs for fast interpretation of results and better comparability of therapies.

Box 11.5   Documentation sheet No. 10: Statistical results

(p_code)   **Patient code (ID code):**   _____

(t_global)   Global *therapist's* estimation for the success of therapy:

Improved					No change		Deteriorated		
5	4	3	2	1	0	−1	− 2	−3	−4	−5

(p_global)   Global *patient's* estimation for the success of therapy on the base of GAS:

Clearly more improvement than expected	Less improvement than expected	Expected outcome	Less deterioration than expected	Clearly more deterioration than expected
2	1	0	−1	−2

(statist)   Were statistical methods used?   Yes/No

(stat_sof)   Which software was used?   _____

Scoring of variable:	Statistical methods:	Result:
(var_1)_____	(var_st1)_____	(var_sig1)_____
(var_2)_____	(var_st2)_____	(var_sig2)_____
(var_3)_____	(var_st3)_____	(var_sig3)_____
(var_4)_____	(var_st4)_____	(var_sig4)_____
(var_5)_____	(var_st5)_____	(var_sig5)_____

The documentation system is complemented by the therapy process graphs (see Figure 11.3), and all documentation sheets now represent a well-documented therapy according to controlled practice (cf. Figure 11.4).

11.3   ELECTRONIC DOCUMENTATION

Fast accessible data is a prerequisite to all kinds of evaluation. For this purpose, the collected information is also stored electronically,

---

Box 11.6   Rules for illustration of the therapy process

1. The complete process shall be presented on a single sheet.
2. The expressions/terms for the process must be clear and unambiguous.
3. The same numeric range of scales must be used in both process graph and questionnaire.
4. Intermissions or missing data name to be indicated (interruption of therapy process).
5. The expectations mentioned by the patient (statements of Actual Condition (AC) vs Specified Condition (SC)) have to be highlighted graphically.
6. Graphical smoothing should occur only in cases with discernible trend present. Other hypotheses of change do not allow for interpolation techniques (e.g. change-invariability).

---

e.g. in SPSS data files. We have prepared those sheets to enable you to use them directly for your data storage (http://www.fire.uni-bremen.de/ZFR). Spreadsheets of different therapists can be connected easily since they display a similar–same structural layout, i.e. number, order, content, and coding of columns. Therefore it is recommended that you abide rigorously by the suggested structure.

We now turn to show how data are input into these spreadsheets. The 12 documentation sheets and the completed questionnaires of the therapy process are good starting points. Part of this information is filed in three different spreadsheets:

- The first spreadsheet includes the *therapy process data* from the questionnaires.
- The second spreadsheet contains *information about the patient* and the therapy.
- The third spreadsheet is composed of *basic conditions* characteristic to a therapy, such as the setting or the therapist attributes.

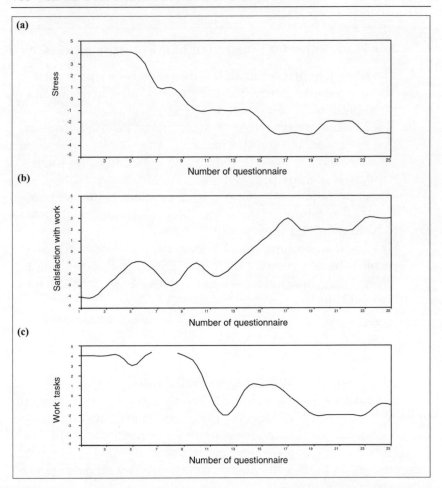

Figure 11.3   Example of therapy process of stress, satisfaction and work quantity (including missing data and a smoothing of the courses)

The first spreadsheet includes the therapy process data of a patient. This information is subject to direct utilization. For every patient a separate spreadsheet must be laid out, and should be in the form shown in Figure 11.5.

The second spreadsheet contains patient data (cf. Box 11.1) as well as therapy features from Box 11.2. Here, details from documentation sheets 1, 5, 9 and 10 are entered. Because of the size of this spreadsheet only its structure is shown. In variable names, the

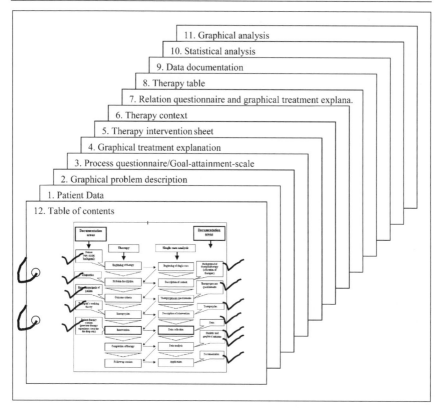

Figure 11.4 A documented therapy according to controlled practice

labels and positions within the SPSS data file are listed. Each variable name is printed next to its item on the documentation sheets. Figure 11.6 shows how the documentation sheet items are transferred to the SPSS spreadsheet.

The third and last spreadsheet (cf. Figure 11.7) contains features of the therapist. Those have to be answered once by the therapist, and be updated at progressively longer time intervals. The corresponding documentation sheet can be found in Box 11.3.

The second and third spreadsheets can be connected for evaluation purposes, so that features of the therapist may be used as common items in all his therapies. It should be possible, then, to compare the successful and unsuccessful therapies of two therapists in order to find common features.

Table 11.1 SPSS table showing the suggested structure of the spreadsheet

Name	Label	Position
p_code	Patient code	1
birth	Date of birth	2
p_sex		3
nation		4
ethno		5
family		6
sibling	Sibling	7
finance	Financial situation	8
job		9
ill		10
illdays	Sick leave days	11
job_load		12
educatio	Education	13
home		14
aggree		15
t_acco	Account of therapy experience	16
t_break	Interrupted therapies	17
b_reason	Reason for interruptions	18
t_begin	Therapy beginning date	19
t_end	Therapy ending date	20
frequenc	Number of meetings	21
interrup	Therapy interruption	22
ending	Regular therapy ending	23
end_c	Reason for therapy termination	24
t_single	Single or group therapy	25
t_financ	Financing of therapy	26
supervis	Supervision in therapy	27
consult	Consulting	28
allianz	Alliance	29
material	Therapy material	30
tec_ins	Technical instrument	31
t_global	Global estimation from the therapist	32
p_global	Global estimation from the patient (GAS)	33
statist	Statistical testing of significance	34
stat_sof	Software for statistical testing	35
var_1	Item 1 of questionnaire	36
var_st1	Statistical test for item 1	37
var_sig1	Significance for item 1	38
var_2	Item 2 of questionnaire	39
var_st2	Statistical test for item 2	40
var_sig2	Significance for item 2	41
etc.		

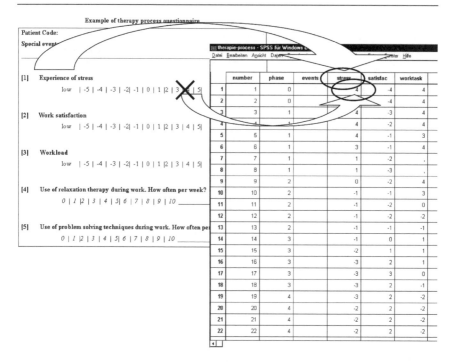

Figure 11.5 Transfer of answers of the therapy process questionnaire to the SPSS spreadsheet

11.4 PROSPECT: META-ANALYSIS OF SINGLE CASES

A documentation system has to be restricted in order to be implemented in a psychotherapist's practice. With the documentation sheets provided, therapeutical behavior can be reconstructed and reviewed. Furthermore, the documentation system offers the following opportunities for comparison:

- different diagnoses groups (e.g. effectiveness of assertiveness training targeting different forms of fear)
- different therapy approaches (e.g. effectiveness of cognitive and psychoanalytical therapy targeting social phobia)
- different therapists (e.g. education and job experience)
- different therapy centers, and
- different structural conditions.

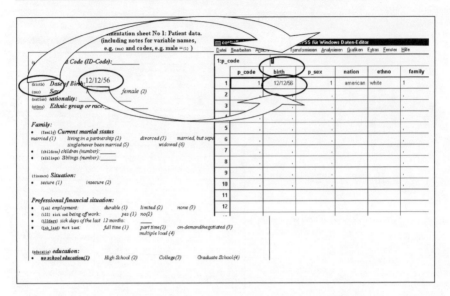

Figure 11.6   Transfer of documentation sheet items to SPSS spreadsheet

Meta-analysis of single-case research has to be seen as a special form of data collection and processing. In clinical practice, accumulated single-case data can be aggregated according to the suggested rules. Unlike the procedure of replication, which has often been recommended as a validation strategy of single-case analysis (cf. Sidman, 1960; Barlow & Hersen, 1984), meta-analysis of single-case research (Faith, Allison & Gorman, 1996) offers the opportunity to compare cases qualitatively.

Replication primarily refers to the comparison of single cases with comparable features (disorder, therapeutical procedure; Sidman, 1960). The aim of replication is to compare single cases, to check results and to apply them to new situations. In 1984, Barlow and Hersen had defined replication as a method of evaluating single-case statements, and the following issues can therefore be evaluated by replication:

- the validity area of single-case results
- evidence of individual case results.

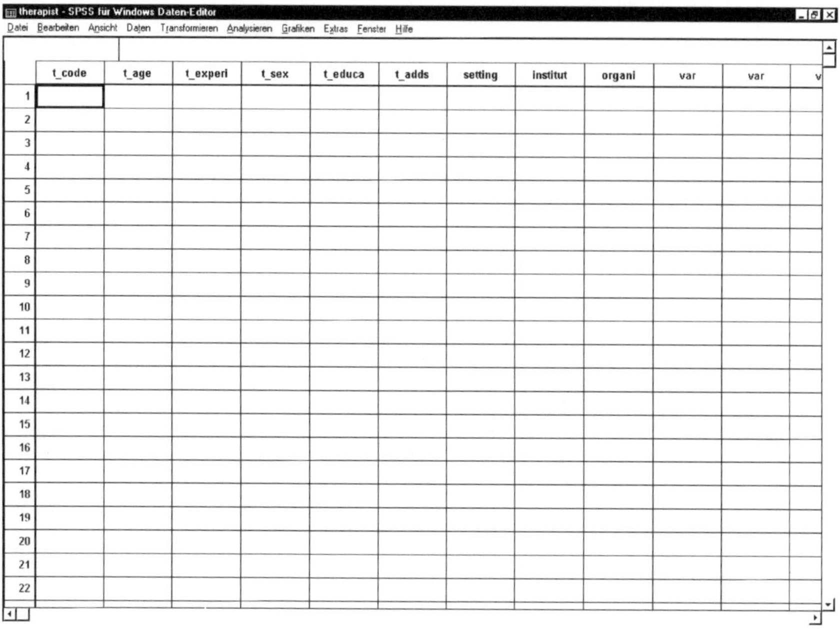

Figure 11.7 Screenshot of SPSS spreadsheet of therapist-specific information

The application of systematic replication in clinical practice performs a transition from practice-oriented therapy control to clinical research.

REFERENCES

Alberts G & Edelstein B (1990) Therapist training: A critical review of skill training studies. *Clinical Psychology Review*. 10 (5): 497–511.

American Psychiatric Association (1994) *Diagnostic and Statistical Manual of Mental Disorders* (4th edn). Washington DC: Author.

Barlow DH (1981) On the relation of clinical research to clinical practice: Current issues, new directions. *Journal of Consulting and Clinical Psychology* 43 (2): 147–55.

Barlow DH & Hersen M (1984) *Single Case Experimental Designs—Strategies for Studying Behavior Chance* (2nd edn). New York: Pergamon Press.

Battle CC, Imber SD, Hoehn-Saric R, Stone AR, Nash, ER & Frank, JD (1966) Target complaints as criterion of improvement. *American Journal of Psychotherapy* 20: 184–92.

Beach S, Sandeen E & O'Leary KD (1990) *Depression in Marriage*. New York: Guilford Press.

Beck AT (1976) *Cognitive Therapy and Emotional Disorder*. New York: International University Press.

Beck AT & Steer RA (1978) *Beck Depression Inventory Manual*. New York: The Psychological Corporation: Harcourt Brace Jovanovich

Beers C (1908) *A Mind that Found Itself: An Autobiography*. New York: Longman Green.

Bem S, Rappard H & van Hoorn W (Eds) (1984) *Studies in the History of Psychology and the Social Science*, Vol. 2. Leiden: Psychologisch Instituut Rijksuniversiteit Leiden, 48–160.

Bereiter C (1963) Some persisting dilemmas in the measurement of change. In C W Harris (Ed.) *Problems in Measuring Change*. Madison: University Wisconsin Press.

Berzins JI (1977) Therapist–patient matching. In AS Gurman & AM Razin (Eds) *Effective Psychotherapy*. New York: Pergamon Press.

Beutler LE (1998) Identifying empirically supported treatments: What if we didn't? *Journal of Consulting and Clinical Psychology* 66 (1): 113–20.

Beutler LE, Wakefield P & Williams RE (1994) Use of psychological tests/ instruments for treatment planning. In M Maruish (Ed.) *Use of Psychological Testing for Treatment Planning and Outcome Assessment*. Hillsdale NJ: Erlbaum.

Bijou, SW & Dunitz-Johnson E (1981) Interbehavior analysis of developmental retardation. *Psychological Record* 31 (3): 305–29.

Boring EG (1929) The psychology of controversy. *Psychological Review* 36: 97–121.

Boring EG (1950) Great men and scientific progress. *Proceedings of the American Philosophical Society* 94: 339–51.

Borkovec TD & Castonguay LG (1998) What is the scientific meaning of empirically supported therapy? *Journal of Consulting and Clinical Psychology* 66 (1): 136–42.

Bortz J & Lienert G (1990) *Verteilungsfreie Methoden in der Biostatistik*. Berlin: Springer.

Bortz J & Lienert GA (1998) *Kurzgefaßte Statistik für die klinische Forschung*. Berlin: Springer.

Box GE & Jenkins GM (1970) *Time Series Analysis: Forecasting and Control*. San Francisco: Holden Day.

Box GE, Jenkins GM & Reinsel GC (1994) *Time Series Analysis: Forecasting and Control*. Englewood Cliffs NJ: Prentice Hall.

Bretano F (1874, repr 1955) *Psychologie vom empirischen Standpunkt*, Vol. 1. Meiner: Hamburg.

Bruch M (1998) UCL case formulation model: clinical applications and procedures. In: M Bruch & Bond F (Eds) *Beyond Diagnosis. Case Formulation Approaches in CBT*. Wiley: Chichester.

Calhoun KS, Moras K, Pilkonis PA & Rehm LP (1998) Empirically supported treatments: Implication for training. *Journal of Consulting and Clinical Psychology* 66 (1): 151–62.

Campbell DT & Stanley JC (1963) *Experimental and Quasi-experimental Design for Research*. Boston: Mifflin.

Cattell RB (1944) Interpretation of the twelve primary personality factors. *Character and Personality* 13: 55–90.

Center for Studying Health Systems Change (2000) Do HMO's make a difference? *Issue Brief: Findings from HSC* 28. Washington DC.

Chamberlin J (1995) Rehabilitating ourselves: The psychiatric survivor movement. *International Journal of Mental Health* 24: 39–46.

Chambless DL & Hollon SD (1998) Defining empirically supported therapies. *Journal of Consulting and Clinical Psychology* 66 (1): 7–18.

Chassan JB (1960) Statistical inference and the single case in clinical design. *Psychiatry. Journal for the Study of Interpersonal Processes* 23: 173–84

Chatfield C (1980) *The Analysis of Time Series*. London: Chapman & Hall.

Clark CA (1963) Hypothesis testing in relation to statistical methodology. *Review of Educational Research* 33: 455–73.

Cochran WG (1954) Some methods for strengthening the common χ^2–tests. *Biometrics* 10: 417–51.

Collingwood RG (1969) *An Essay in Metaphysics*. Oxford: Clarendon Press.

Conoley JC & Impara JC (Eds) (1995) *The Twelfth Mental Measurements Yearbook*. Lincoln: University of Nebraska Press.

Cook TD & Campbell DT (1979). *Quasi-Experimentation: Design and Analysis Issues for Field Settings*. Chicago: Rand McNally.

Corcoran K & Fischer J (1994) *Measures for Clinical Practice: A Sourcebook*. New York: Macmillan.

Cronbach LJ (1975) Beyond the two disciplines of scientific psychology. *American Psychologist* 30 (2): 116–27.

Cronbach LJ & Furby L (1970) How we should measure 'change': Or should we? *Psychological Bulletin* 74 (1): 68–80.

Crosbie J (1993) Interrupted time series analysis with brief single subject data. *Journal of Consulting and Clinical Psychology* 61: 966–74.

Danzinger K (1990) *Constructing the Subject: Historical Origins of Psychological Research*. New York: Cambridge University Press.

David FN (1950) Two combinatorial tests of whether a sample has come from a given population. *Biometrika* 37: 97–110.

DeJong G & Sutton G (1995) Rehab 2000: The evolution of medical rehabilitation in American healthcare. In P Kitchell Landrum, ND Schmidt & A McLean (Eds) *Outcome Oriented Rehabilitation: Principles, Strategies, and Tools for Effective Program Management*. Gaithersburg: Aspen.

Diamond F (1998) You can drag physicians to guidelines . . . but you can't make them comply (mostly). Retrieved 17 February 2000 from the World Wide Web: http://www.managedcaremag.com/archiveMC/9809/9809.carrot.shtml

Donabedian A (1966) Evaluating the quality of managed care. *Milbank Memorial Fund Quarterly* 3 (Suppl): 166–206.

Dougher MJ & Hackbert L (1994) A behavior-analytic account of depression and a case report using acceptance-based procedures. *Behavior Analyst* 17 (2): 321–34.

Drucker P (1964) *How to manage by results*. New York: Harper.

Dukes WF (1965) $N = 1$. *Psychological Bulletin* 64 (1): 74–9.

Duncker K (1935, repr 1974) *Zur Psychologie des produktiven Denkens*. Berlin: Springer.

Ebbinghaus H (1885) *Über das Gedächtnis*. Leipzig.

Eimer M (1987) *Konzepte von Kausalität*. Bern: Huber.

Elliott R & Wexler MM (1994) Measuring the impact of sessions in process-experiential therapy of depression: The Session Impacts Scale. *Journal of Counseling Psychology* 41: 166–74.

Ellis A (1973) *Humanistic psychology: The Rational – Emotive Approach*. New York: McGraw-Hill.

Eysenck HJ (1944) Types of personality—a factorial study of 700 neurotics. *Journal of Mental Science* 90: 851–61.

Eysenck HJ (1947) *Dimensions of Personality*. London: Routledge & Kegan Paul.

Eysenck HJ (1952) The effects of psychotherapy: An evaluation. *Journal of Consulting Psychology* 16: 319–24.

Eysenck HJ (1953) *The Structure of Human Personality*. London: Methuen.

Faith MS, Allison DB & Gorman BS (1996) Meta-analysis of single-case research. In RD Franklin, DB Allison & BS Gorman (Eds) *Design and Analysis of Single-Case Research*. Hillsdale NJ: Erlbaum.

Farnum NR & Stanton LW (1989) *Quantitative Forecasting Methods*. Boston: PWS-Kent Publishing Company.

Fishman DB (2000) Transcending the efficacy versus effectiveness research debate: Proposal for a new, electronic 'Journal of Pragmatic Case Studies'. *Prevention & Treatment* 3, Article 8. Retrieved 3 August 2000 from the World Wide Web: http://journals.apa.org/prevention/volume3/pre0030008a.html

Ford JD (1979) Research on training counselors and clinicians. *Review of Educational Research* 49 (1): 87–130.

Franklin RD, Allison DB & Gorman BS (Eds) (1997) *Design and Analysis of Single-Case Research*. New Jersey: Lawrence Erlbaum.

Franklin RD, Gorman BS, Beasley TM & Allison DB (1996) Graphical display and visual analysis. In RD Franklin, DB Allison & BS Gorman (Eds) *Design and Analysis of Single-Case Research*. Mahwah NJ: Erlbaum.

Freud S & Breuer J (1895, repr 1970) *Studien über Hysterie*. Frankfurt: Fisher.

Galano J (1977) Treatment effectiveness as a function of client involvement in goal-setting and goal-planning. *Goal Attainment Review* 3: 17–32.

Galotti KM (1999) *Cognitive Psychology: In and Out of the Laboratory*. Belmont CA: Brooks/Cole Wadsworth.

Garfield SL (1980) *Psychotherapy. An Eclectic Approach*. New York: Wiley.

Garfield, SL (1982) Eclecticism and integration in psychotherapy. *Behavior-Therapy* 13 (5): 610–23.

Garfield SL & Bergin AE (1994) Introduction and historical overview. In AE Bergin & SL Garfield (Eds) *Handbook of Psychotherapy and Behavior Change*. New York: Wiley.

Garfield SL (1998) Some comments on empirically supported treatments. *Journal of Consulting and Clinical Psychology* 66 (1): 121–5.

Gilchrist W (1984) *Statistical Modeling*. London: Wiley.

Glass GV, Wilson VL & Gottman JM (1975) Design and analysis of time-series experiments. Boulder Colorado: Association University Press.

Goldman HH & Morrissey JP (1985) The alchemy of mental health policy: Homelessness and the fourth cycle of reform. *American Journal of Public Health* 75: 727–31.

Goldman W (1997) *Goal Focused Treatment Planning and Outcomes*. Minneapolis MN: United Behavioral Health.

Goldman W, McCulloch J & Sturm R (1998) Costs and use of mental health services before and after managed care. *Health Affairs* (Millwood) 17: 40–52.

Gorman BS & Allison DB (1996) Statistical alternatives for single-case designs. In RD Franklin, DB Allison & BS Gorman (Eds) *Design and Analysis of Single-Case Research*. Mahwah NJ: Erlbaum.

Gottman JM (1981) *Time Series Analysis*. Cambridge: Cambridge University Press.

Gresham FM (1996) Treatment integrity in single-subject research. In RD Franklin, DB Allison & BS Gorman (Eds) *Design and Analysis of Single-Case Research*. Mahwah NJ: Lawrence Erlbaum.

Grob GN (1983) *Mental Illness and American Society, 1875–1940*. Princeton NJ: Princeton University Press.

Grob GN (1991) *From Asylum to Community: Mental Health Policy in Modern America*. Princeton NJ: Princeton University Press.

Grob GN (1994) *The Mad Among Us: A History of the Care of America's Mentally Ill*. New York: Free Press.

Guilford JP (1940) *Manual for an Inventory of Factors STDCR*. Beverly Hills: Sheridan Supply.

Gurin J, Veroff J & Feld S (1960) *Americans View their Mental Health: A Nationwide Interview Survey* (A report to the staff director, Jack R Ewalt). New York: Basic Books.

Guy W (Ed) (1976) *ECDEU Assessment Manual for Psychopharmacology—Revised*. Rockville: NIMH.

Hagopian LP, Fisher WW, Thompson RH, Owen DeSchryver J, Iwata BA & Wacker DP (1997) Toward the development of structured criteria for interpretation of functional analysis data. *Journal of Applied Behavior Analysis* 30 (2): 313–26.

Harris CW (Ed) (1963) *Problems in Measuring Change*. Madison: University Wisconsin Press.

Hart HLA & Honoré AM (1973) *Causation in the Law* (reprint). Oxford: Clarendon Press.

Haynes SN (1993) Treatment Implications of psychological assessment. *Psychological Assessment* 5 (3): 251–3.

Haynes SN (1998) The assessment–treatment relationship and functional analysis in behavior therapy. *European Journal of Psychological Assessment* 14 (1): 26–35.

Haynes SN (1998) The changing nature of behavioral assessment. In AS Bellack & M Hersen (Eds) *Behavioral Assessment A Practical Handbook*. Boston: Allyn and Bacon.

Haynes SN, Leisen MB & Blaine DD (1997) Design of individualized behavioral treatment programs using functional analytic clinical case models. *Psychological Assessment* 9 (4): 334–48.

Haynes SN & O'Brian WO (1990) The functional analysis in behavior therapy. *Clinical Psychology Review* 10: 649–68.

Haynes SN, Spain EH & Oliveira J (1993) Identifying causal relationships in clinical assessment. *Psychological Assessment* 5 (3): 281–91.

Hays W (1970) *Statistics for the Social Sciences*. New York: Holt, Rinehart & Winston.

Hazelett R & Haynes SN (1992) Fibromyalgia: A time-series analysis of the stressor-physical symptom association. *Journal of Behavioral Medicine* 15: 541–58.

Herson DH & Barlow DH (1984) *Single-Case Experimental Designs: Strategies for Studying Behavior Change*. New York: Pergamon Press.

Hilliard RB (1993) Single-case methodology in psychotherapy process and outcome research. *Journal of Consulting and Clinical Psychology* 61 (3): 373–80.

Hollins CR & Trower P (Eds) (1986) *Handbook of Social Skills Training*. New York: Pergamon.

Houts P & Scott R (1976) Goal planning in mental health rehabilitation. *Goal Attainment Review* 2: 33–51.

Howard KI & Orlinsky DE (1972) Psychotherapeutic processes. *Annual Review of Psychology* 615–68.

Hughes JN & Sullivan KA (1988) Outcome assessment in social skills training with children. *Journal of School Psychology* 26: 167–83.

Hume D (1738) Abstract of 'A Treatise of Humane Nature'.

Huynh H & Feldt L (1970) Conditions under which mean square ratios in repeated measurement designs have exact F-distributions. *Journal of the American Statistical Association* 65: 1582–9.

ISO (1998) Selection and Use of ISO 9000, retrieved 17 February 2000 from the World Wide Web: http://www.iso.ch/9000e/9k14ke.htm

ISO (2000) ISO-9000, retrieved 17 February 2000 from the World Wide Web:

http://www.tc176.org/faqs/index.html

Iwata BA, Pace GM, Dorsey MF, Zarcone JF, Vollmer TR, Smith RG et al. (1994) The function of self-injurious behavior: An experimental-epidemiological analysis. *Journal of Applied Behavior Analysis* 26: 215–39.

Jacobs S & Cytrynbaum S (1977) The Goal Attainment Scale: A test of its use in an inpatient crisis intervention unit. *Goal Attainment Review* 3: 77–98.

Jacobson E (1938) *Progressive Relaxation*. Chicago: University of Chicago Press.

Jaspers K (1913, repr 1946) *Allgemeine Psychopathologie*. Berlin: Springer.

Jones E, Ghannam J, Nigg JT & Dyer JFP (1993) A paradigm for single-case research: The time series study of a long-term psychotherapy for depression. *Journal of Consulting and Clinical Psychology* 61 (3): 381–94.

Jones RSP & Heskins KJ (1988) Toward a functional analysis of delinquent behavior: A pilot study. *Counselling Psychology Quarterly* 1: 33–42.

Kazdin AE (1982) *Single-Case Research Designs: Methods for Clinical and Applied Settings*. New York: Oxford University Press.

Kazdin AE (1984) Statistical analyses for single-case experimental designs. In DH Barlow & M Hersen (Eds) *Single-Case Experimental Designs*. New York: Pergamon Press.

Kazdin AE (1997) A model for developing effective treatments: Progression and interplay of theory, research and practice. *Journal of Clinical Child Psychology* 26 (2): 114–29.

Kazdin AE (1998) Drawing valid inferences from case studies. In AE Kazdin (Ed) *Methodological Issues and Strategies in Clinical Research*. Washington DC: American Psychological Association.

Kanfer FH & Busemeyer JR (1982) The use of problem solving and decision making in behavior therapy. *Clinical Psychology Review* 2 (2): 239–66.

Kanfer FH & Goldstein AP (1991) Introduction. In FH Kanfer & AP Goldstein (Eds) *Helping People Change: A Textbook of Methods*. New York: Pergamon Press.

Kanfer FH & Saslow G (1969) Behavioral diagnosis. In CM Franks (Eds) *Behavioral Therapy: Appraisal and Status*. New York: McGraw Hill.

Karasu TB (1986) The specificity versus nonspecificity dilemma: Toward identifying therapeutic change agents. *American Journal of Psychiatry* 143 (6): 687–95.

Katz J, Ritvo P, Irvine MJ & Jackson M (1996) Coping with chronic pain. In M Zeidner & NS Endler (Eds) *Handbook of Coping*. New York: Wiley.

Kearney CA & Silverman WK (1990) A preliminary analysis of a functional model of assessment and treatment for school refusal behavior. *Behavior-Modification* 14 (3): 340–66.

Kelley HH (1973) The process of causal attribution. *American Psychologist* 28: 107–28.

Kelly GA (1955) *The Psychology of Personal Constructs* (I, II). New York: Norton.

Kelly GA (1958) Man's construction of his alternatives. In G Lindzey (Ed) *Assessment of Human Motives*. New York: Rinehart.

Kendall PC (1998) Empirically supported therapies. *Journal of Consulting and Clinical Psychology* 66 (1): 3–6.

Kendall PC, Flannery Schroeder E & Ford J (1999) Therapy outcome research methods. In PC Kendall, JN Butcher & GN Hombeck (Eds) *Handbook of Research Methods in Clinical Psychology*. New York: Wiley.

Keyser DJ & Sweetland RC (Eds) (1985) *Test critiques (1)*. Kansas City: Test Corporation of America.

Kiesler DJ (1966) Some myths of psychotherapy research and the search for a paradigm. *Psychological Bulletin* 65 (2): 110–36.

Kiresuk TJ & Sherman RE (1968) Goal Attainment Scaling: A general method for evaluating comprehensive community mental health programs. *Community Mental Health Journal* 4 (6): 443–53.

Kiresuk TJ, Smith A & Cardillo JE (Eds) (1994) *Goal Attainment Scaling: Applications, Theory and Measurement.* New Jersey: Lawrence Erlbaum.

Kratochwill TR & Levin JR (Eds) (1992) *Single-Case Research Design and Analysis. New Directions for Psychology and Education.* New Jersey: Lawrence Erlbaum.

Krauth J (1990) Comments on the paper by Möller et al. (1989): Problems in single-case evaluation. *Eur Arch Psychiatry Neurol Sci* 239 (6): 391–4; discussion 395–7

Laferriere L & Callsyn R (1977) GAS: An effective treatment technique in short-term therapy. *American Journal of Community Psychology* 6: 271–82.

Latané B & Darley JM (1970) *The Unresponsive Bystander: Why Doesn't He Help?* New York: Appleton-Century-Cofts.

Lautsch E & Lienert GA (1993) *Binärdatenanalyse.* Weinheim: PVU.

Lefley HP (1996) Impact of consumer and family advocacy movement on mental health services. In BL Levin & J Petrila (Eds) *Mental Health Services: A Public Health Perspective.* New York: Oxford University Press, 81–96.

Linden M (1987) *Phase-IV-Forschung.* Berlin: Springer.

Luborsky L (1984) *Principles of Psychoanalytic Psychotherapy: A Manual for Supportive-Expressive Treatment.* New York: Basic Books.

Luborsky L, Crits-Christoph P, Mintz J & Auerbach A (1988) *Who will Benefit from Psychotherapy?* New York: Basic Books.

Lyons JS, Howard KI, O'Mahoney MT & Lish JD (1997) *The Measurement and Management of Clinical Outcomes in Mental Health.* New York: Wiley.

Mace FC & West BJ (1986) Unresolved theoretical issues in self-management: Implications for research and practice. *Professional School Psychology* 1 (3): 149–63.

Malan DH (1963) *A Study of Brief Psychotherapy.* London: Tavistock Clinic.

Mash EJ & Hunsley J (1993) Assessment considerations in the identification of failing psychotherapy: Bringing the negatives out of the darkroom. *Psychological Assessment* 5: 292–301.

McDowall D, McCleary R, Meidinger EE & Hay AR (1980) *Interrupted Time Series Analyses.* Beverly Hills: Sage.

Meichenbaum D (1977) *Cognitive-Behavior Modification.* New York: Plenum Press.

Meyer V (1957) Case report the treatment of two phobic patients on the basis of learning principles. *The Journal of Abnormal and Social Psychology* 55: 261–6.

Meyer V & Turkat ID (1979) Behavioral analysis of clinical cases. *Journal of Behavioral Assessment* 1: 259–69.

Meyer-Bahlburg HFL (1969) Spearmans rho als punktbiserialer Rangkorrelationskoeffizient. *Biometrische Zeitschrift* 11: 60–6.

Michotte A (1963) *The Perception of Causality.* London: Methuen.

Mitscherlich A (1947) *Vom Ursprung der Sucht.* Stuttgart: Klett.

Morrissey JP & Goldman HH (1985) Cycles of reform in the care of the chronically mentally ill. *Hospital and Community Psychiatry* 35: 785–93.

Müller J (1833–1840, Engl. 1942) *Handbuch der Physiologie des Menschen.* Coblenz: Holscher.

National Association of State Mental Health Program Directors (1993) *Putting their Money where their Mouths are: SMHA Support of Consumer and Family-run Programs.* Arlington VA: Author.

National Institute of Health (1999) *Almanac*. Retrieved 17 February 2000 from the World Wide Web: http://www.nih.gov/about/almanac/index.html

National Institute of Mental Health (1999) *Mental Health: A Report. Surgeons General*. Retrieved 17 February 2000 from the World Wide Web: http://www.nimh.nih.gov/mhsgrpt/home.html

Newman FL & Ciarlo JA (1994) Criteria for selecting psychological instruments for treatment outcome assessment. In ME Maruish (Ed): *The Use of Psychological Testing for Treatment Planning and Outcome Assessment*. Hillsdale: Erlbaum.

Orlinsky DE & Howard KI (1975) *Varieties of Psychotherapeutic Experience: Multivariate Analyses of Patients' and Therapists' Reports*. New York: Teachers College Press.

Parsonson BS & Baer DM (1978) The analysis and presentation of graphic data. In TR Kratochwill (Ed) *Single Subject Design*. New York: Academic Press.

Paul GL (1967) Strategy of outcome research in psychotherapy. *Journal of Consulting Psychology* 31: 109–18.

Penn DL & Martin J (1998) The stigma of severe mental illness: Some potential solutions for a recalcitrant problem. *Psychiatric Quarterly* 69: 235–47.

Petermann F (1982) *Einzelfalldiagnostik in der klinischen Praxis*. Weinheim: PVU.

Pfanzagl J (1994) *Allgemeine Methodenlehre der Statistik, Bd II*. Berlin: de Gruyter.

Phelan J, Link B, Stueve A & Pescosolido B (1997, August) *Public conceptions of mental illness in 1950 in 1996: Has sophistication increased? Has stigma declined*? Paper presented at the meeting of the American Sociological Association. Toronto, Ontario.

Piaget J (1952) *The Origins of Intelligence in Children*. New York: International University Press.

Preyer W (1882) *Die Seele des Kindes. Beobachtungen über die geistige Entwicklung des Menschen in den ersten Lebensjahren*. Leipzig.

Quetelet LA (1835, Engl. 1969) *Sur l'homme et le développement de ses facultés*. Paris: Bachelier. (Engl. title: *A Treatise on Man and the Development of His Faculties*. Gainesville, Fla: Scholars' Facsimiles.)

Regier D, Goldberg I & Taube C (1978) The de facto US mental health services system: A public health perspective. *Archives of General Psychiatry* 35: 685–93.

Regier DA, Narrow W, Rae DS, Manderscheid RW, Locke BZ & Goodwin FK (1993) The de facto US mental and addictive disorders service system. Epidemiologic Catchment Area prospective 1-year prevalence rates of disorders and services. *Archives of General Psychiatry* 50: 85–94.

Revusky H (1967) Some statistical treatments compatible with individual organism methodology. *Journal of the Experimental Analysis of Behavior* 10: 319–30.

Rickels K & Hesbacher P (1969) The private practice research group: Cooperative efforts in drug evaluation. *Psychopharmacology Bulletin* 5 (4): 22–4.

Rosenthal R (1991) *Meta-analytical Procedures for Social Research*. Newbury Park: Sage.

Rosenthal R & Harris MJ (1985) Mediation of interpersonal expectancy effects: 31 meta-analyses. *Psychological Bulletin* 97: 363–86.

Rotter JB (1954, 1934) *Social Learning and Clinical Psychology*. Englewood Cliffs NJ: Prentice Hall.

Sameroff A & Chandler M (1975) Reproductive risk and the continuum of caretaking causality. *Review of Child Development Research* 4: 187–244.

Seaberg JR & Gillespie DF (1977) Goal Attainment Scaling: A critique. *Social Work Research and Abstracts* 13: 4–11.

Seligman MEP (2000) Comment on Fishman's 'Transcending the Efficacy versus effectiveness research debate'. *Prevention & Treatment* 3, Article 11. Retrieved 3 August 2000 from the World Wide Web: http://journals.apa.org/prevention/volume3/pre00300011c.html

Shapiro DH (1990) Clinical applications of a control model of psychological health: Two case studies of stress-related disorders. *Psychotherapy Patient* 7 (1–2): 169–98.

Shapiro MB (1961) A method of measuring psychological changes specific to the individual psychiatric patient. *British Journal of Medical Psychology* 34: 151–5.

Shiffman S (1987) Clinical psychology training and psychotherapy interview performance. *Psychotherapy* 24 (1): 71–84.

Shine LC & Bower SM (1971) A one-way analysis of variance for single-subject designs. *Educational and Psychological Measurement* 31: 105–13.

Sidman M (1960) *Tactics of Scientific Research*. New York: Basic Books.

Slade PD (1982) Towards a functional analysis of anorexia nervosa and bulimia nervosa. *British Journal of Clinical Psychology* 21 (3): 167–79.

Smith ML, Glass VG & Miller TI (1980) *The benefits of psychotherapy*. Baltimore: Johns Hopkins University Press.

South Carolina SHARE (1995) *National Directory of Mental Health Consumer and Ex-patient Organizations and Resources*. Charlotte SC: Author.

Star SA (1952) *What the public thinks about mental health and mental illness*. Paper presented at the annual meeting of the National Association for Mental Health.

Star SA (1955) *The public's ideas about mental illness*. Paper presented at the annual meeting of the National Association for Mental Health.

Startup M & Shapiro DA (1993) Therapist treatment fidelity in prescriptive vs exploratory psychotherapy. *British Journal of Clinical Psychology* 32: 443–56.

Stern W (1911) *Differentielle Psychologie in ihren methodischen Grundlagen*. Leipzig: Barth.

Stevens WL (1939) Distribution of groups in a sequence of alternatives. *Annals of Eugenics* 8: 10–17.

Stiles WB, Reynolds S, Hardy GE & Rees A (1994) Evaluation and description of psychotherapy sessions by clients using the Session *Evaluation Questionnaire and the Session Impacts Scale. Journal of Counseling Psychology* 41: 175–85.

Stiles WB, Shapiro DA & Elliott R (1986) Are all psychotherapies equivalent? *American Psychologist* 41 (2): 165–80.

Stratton GM (1897) Vision without inversion of the retinal image. *Psychological Review* 4: 341–60.

Stricker G (2000) The relationship between efficacy and effectiveness. *Prevention and Treatment* 3, Article 8. Retrieved 3 August 2000 from the World Wide Web: http://journals.apa.org/prevention/volume3/pre0030010c.html

Strupp HH (1993) The Vanderbilt Psychotherapy Studies: Synopsis. *Journal of Consulting and Clinical Psychology* 61 (3): 431–3.

Suchman EA (1967) *Evaluate Research*. New York: Russel Sage Foundation.

Sweetland RC & Keyser DJ (1991) *Tests. A Comprehensive Reference for Assessments in Psychology, Education and Business*. Texas: Pro Ed.

Teska PT (1947) The mentality of hydrocephalics and a description of an interesting case. *Journal of Psychology* 23: 197–203.

Vandereycken W & Meermann R (1988) Chronic illness behavior and non-compliance with treatment: Pathways to an interactional approach. *Psychotherapy and Psychosomatics* (4): 182–91.

Veroff J, Douvan E & Kulka RA (1981) *Mental Health in America: Patterns of Help-Seeking from 1957 to 1976.* New York: Basic Books.

Vervaeke GAC & Emmelkamp PM (1998): Treatment selection: What do we know? *European Journal of Psychological Assesment* 14 (1): 50–9.

Waldmann HC (1997) *Sozialwissenschaftliche Methoden in der klinischen Forschung.* Frankfurt/Main: Lang.

Waldmann HC & Petermann F (1998) Multiple group comparisons: quasi-experimental designs. In AS Barlow & M Hersen (Eds) *Comprehensive Clinical Psychology.* Oxford: Elsevier.

Wallerstein RS, Robbins LL, Luborsky L, Fabian M, Hall BH, Ticho E, Ticho GR, Sargent HD & Modlin H (1958) The psychotherapy research project of the Menninger Foundation: Second report. *Bulletin of the Menninger Clinic* 22: 117–66.

Wallerstein RS, Robbins LL, Sargent HD & Luborsky L (1956) The psychotherapy research project of the Menninger Foundation. *Bulletin of the Menninger Clinic* 20: 221–78.

Wallis WA & Moore GH (1941) A significance test for time series analysis. *Journal of the American Statistical Association* 20: 257–67.

Waltz J, Addis ME, Koerner K & Jacobson NS (1993) Testing the integrity of a Psychotherapy Protocol: Assessment of Adherence and Competence. *Journal of Constulting and Clinical Psychology* 61 (4): 620–30.

Warnock JK, Mintz SI & Twemlow SW (1979) Single-case documentation of psychiatric treatment effectiveness. *Bulletin of the Menninger Clinic* 43 (2): 137–44.

Watson JB & Rayner R (1920) Conditioned emotional reactions. *Journal of Experimental Psychology* 3: 1–14.

Weizäcker V von (1951) *Der kranke Mensch.* Stuttgart: Klett.

White OR (1972) *A manual for the calculation of the median slope: A technique of progress estimation and prediction in the single case.* Working paper No 16. Regional Resource Center for Handicapped Children, University of Oregon, Eugene: Oregon.

White OR (1974) *The 'split middle': A 'quickie' method of trend estimation.* Unpublished manuscript. University of Washington, Experimental Education Unit, Child Development and Mental Retardation Center. Seattle: University of Washington.

Wilson GT (1996) Manual-based treatments: The clinical application of research findings. *Behavioral Research Therapy* 34 (4): 295–314.

Wolf FM (1980) *Meta-analysis: Quantitative Methods for Research Synthesis.* Beverly Hills: Sage.

World Health Organization (1990) ICD-10, September 1990 Draft of Chapter V (F), Categories F00-F99, Mental and Behavioral Disorders (including disorders of psychological development), Diagnostic Criteria for Research, Geneva: WHO (WHO/NMH/MEP 89.1 Rev2).

Wundt W (1974) *Grundzüge der physiologischen Psychologie.* Engelmann: Leipzig.

Yeaton WH & Sechrest L (1981) Meaningful measures of effect. *Journal of Consulting and Clinical Psychology* 49 (5): 766–7.

Yin RK (1984) *Case Study Research: Design and Methods.* Beverly Hills: Sage Publications.

Yin RK (1989) *Case Study Research: Design and Methods* (2nd edn). Newbury Park CA: Sage.

Zubin J (1950) Symposium on statistics for the clinician. *Journal of Clinical Psychology* 6 (1): 1–6.

INDEX